OXFORDSHIRE
COUNTRY WALKS

2

CHILTERNS

TEN CIRCULAR WALKS 3–7 MILES

Mary Webb, Alan Spicer
and Allister Smith

OXFORDSHIRE BOOKS

First published in 1990 by Oxfordshire Books

Copyright © 1990 Oxfordshire County Council

ISBN 1–873222–01–7

British Library Cataloguing-in-publication Data
CIP Catalogue Record for this book is available from the British Library

Typesetting by PM Typesetting Ltd, Exeter

Printed in Great Britain by The Bath Press, Avon

OXFORDSHIRE BOOKS
Official Publisher to Oxfordshire County Council

An imprint of Wheaton Publishers Ltd
A member of Maxwell Communication Corporation plc

Wheaton Publishers Ltd
Hennock Road, Marsh Barton, Exeter, Devon EX2 8RP
Tel: 0392 411131 Fax: 0392 425274
SALES
Direct sales enquiries to Oxfordshire Books at the address above

PREFACE

This series of circular walks covers part of the Oxfordshire Chilterns AONB from Aston Rowant in the north, south-west along the escarpment as far as Swyncombe and Cuxham, then over the plateau towards Henley-on-Thames. Several trails incorporate part of the Oxfordshire Way long distance footpath.

The length of the walks varies between three and seven miles (5 to 11 km) and short cuts are included where possible. There are a few steep climbs but for the most part the going is fairly easy. Obviously the time taken to follow the walks will vary with the individual, but they are designed to be taken at a leisurely pace allowing plenty of time to read the descriptions and look at the landscape and wildlife. Ordnance Survey maps 1:25000 scale will add to the interest of the walks.

This guide has been produced with the aim of showing just how much of our heritage is present in the landscape. You will see features ranging from prehistoric tracks, Domesday Book manors, medieval woodland clearance settlements, eighteenth-century parkland, nineteenth-century fieldscapes and roads and twentieth-century developments. Wildlife can be found everywhere, sometimes in the least obvious places, and often with a tale to tell about the past. The introduction gives a brief background to the history of the landscape and to the origins of its flora and fauna.

We hope you enjoy discovering your landscape as much as we enjoyed producing this book.

ACKNOWLEDGEMENTS

This booklet was written and researched by
Mary Webb, Alan Spicer and Allister Smith, all of the Oxford Polytechnic,
with illustrations by Louise Spicer. The authors are grateful
for help and support from the following organizations:

Oxfordshire County Museum Services; Berks, Bucks and Oxon Naturalists' Trust.

The project was sponsored by Oxfordshire County Council
and South Oxfordshire District Council.

CONTENTS

INTRODUCTION

TEN CIRCULAR WALKS

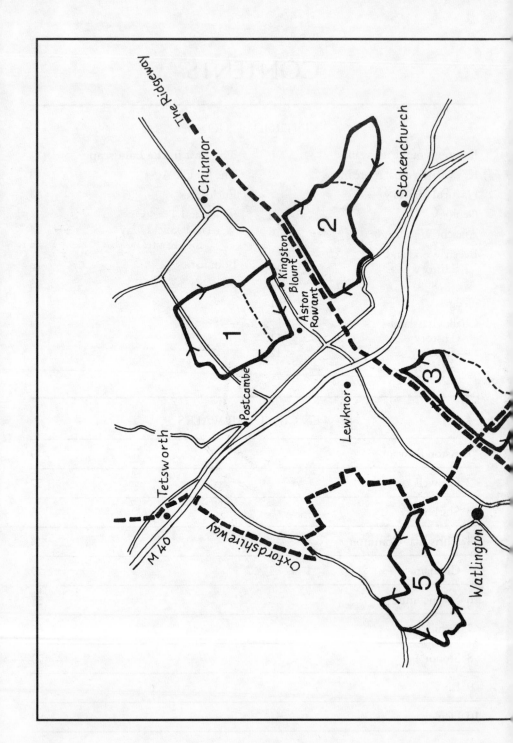

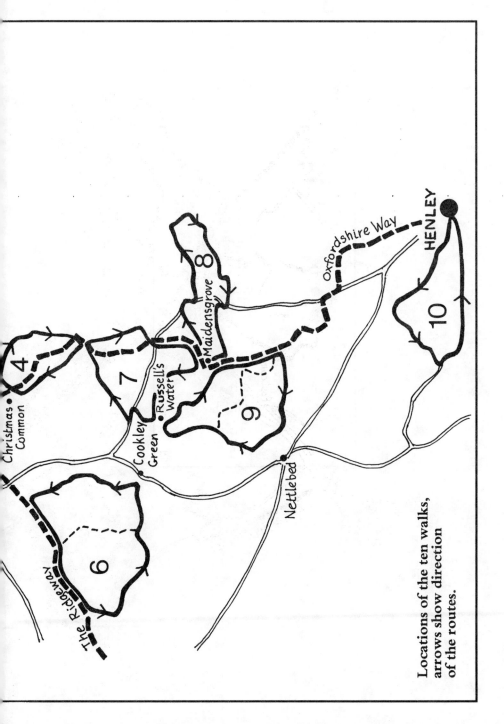

Locations of the ten walks, arrows show direction of the routes.

7

———————	Road
▬ ▬ ▬ ▬	Circular Walk
▬▬▬▬▬▬	Walk on road
———————	Track
- - - - -	Footpath
～～～	Stream
⬯	Pond or lake
▪	Building
⬡	Deciduous trees
⋏	Conifers
⸛	Grassland
+	Church
PH	Public House
NT	National Trust
Spr	Spring

Key to individual route maps

INTRODUCTION

Natural History

GEOLOGY

The Chiltern hills are composed of chalk which is overlain on the hill tops by clay and sometimes sand or gravel. Chalk is made up of the remains of microscopic marine creatures with calcite (calcium based) skeletons which were deposited as mud in a shallow sea, eventually forming very thick layers of chalk. This happened about 100 million years ago in the Cretaceous period.

There are three distinct layers of chalk. Lower chalk is a mixture of clay and chalk, used for cement and, in the past, as marl for improving poor agricultural land. Middle chalk is more pure and contains few flints, while Upper chalk is very white and pure but contains more flint. Flint is formed from silica and is dark-coloured inside with a white coating on exposed surfaces due to loss of water.

The hills themselves were formed at the same time as the Alps when the continental plates of Africa and Europe collided about twenty-six million years ago. The area now making up the south-east of England buckled and a series of east–west folds was formed, one of which was the Chiltern hills. Both before and after this occurrence the area was covered with water which left behind the clay, capping the chalk and the deposits of gravel and sand which are to be found scattered over the region.

During the last two million years, there have been periods of intense cold, with warmer interglacials, the last Ice Age ending about 10000 years ago. The Chiltern region was never covered by ice but was in the grip of periglacial conditions with the ground frozen to great depths and only the surface thawing in the short summers. This temperature difference led to much erosion as the top layers of chalk, shattered by freezing, gradually slid downhill. A feature of many Chiltern valleys is their asymmetry with south-or west-facing slopes being steeper than those facing north or east, and this is thought to be another result of alternate freezing and thawing. The frost action caused the clay deposits to mix with the weathered surface of Upper chalk resulting in the clay-with-flints soil which is present on today's hill tops. This geology is evident in the traditional brick and flint buildings of the Chilterns, making use of readily available materials.

Chalk is extremely porous and can hold much water but because the pores are very small the water tends to remain stationary. However the numerous cracks and fissures allow rain water to permeate down to the water table. Along the bottom of the Chiltern escarpment there are numerous springs where this water meets a layer of more impermeable Upper Greensand and Gault clay. This 'springline' is marked by a string of settlements like Crowell, Shirburn and Pyrton, whose sites were chosen in the distant past because of the presence of water.

ANCIENT WOODLAND

The natural vegetation in southern England, had it been left undisturbed, would now be woodland. After the end of the Ice Age, about ten thousand years ago, 'wild wood', as it is called, covered much of the country but owing to man's increasing impact over the centuries, it was cleared in most places to make way for settled agriculture. The landscape two thousand years ago was similar to that of today in terms of woodland cover. The remaining woodland areas were managed to provide useful timber. Descendants from the original woodland are called primary ancient woodland and are rare. Some present day woodland has grown up in places which at some time in the past has been cleared; if it dates from before 1600 AD it is called secondary ancient woodland. More recent woods are called secondary woodland.

Most of these old areas of woodland were managed by selective felling and coppicing, which is the periodic cutting of the trees to ground level. New growth springs up producing within a few years, wood suitable for fencing, firewood or repairs. Coppicing was used until this century, but with the advent of cheap timber from abroad and reduction in the everyday use of wood this practice has died out in most places.

These methods resulted in a long-term continuity of woodland cover, which encouraged the development of a specific community of plants which can thrive in shady conditions or take advantage of the extra light in the periodic open phases following coppicing or storm damage as has recently happened. These 'indicators' of ancient woodland only spread slowly and so are evidence of a long continuity of woodland cover. Such plants as wood anemone, spurge laurel, goldilocks, wood spurge, sanicle, woodruff and wood sorrel are all good indicator species, but several of these or other typical indicators have to be present in order to positively identify ancient woodland.

BEECH WOODLAND

History

The most striking characteristic of the Chiltern hills is their beech woods. Beech is a native British tree which became widespread in woodland about two and a half thousand years ago, south of a line between the Wash and South Wales. In the past other species such as oak and ash would have been more numerous, but it seems likely that beech was dominant especially on the chalky slopes. Although some experts maintain that all the beech woods were planted for the nineteenth-century furniture industry in High Wycombe, medieval records, like those from Cuxham, point to the plentiful supply of beech. Early travellers like John Leyland and Daniel Defoe in the sixteenth and seventeenth centuries describe the Chiltern beech woods, emphasizing their main use in providing fuel for London by means of coppicing.

As the need for firewood decreased owing to the availability of coal, so beech became the staple for a new local industry, that of furniture making, and management changed to produce timber instead of coppice wood. Over a period of about a century the best trees were felled on a selective basis and used for making the legs and stretchers for Windsor or other chairs which were produced on a large scale in the High Wycombe and Stokenchurch areas.

The timber was cut by hand into logs or planks using seven-foot saws used by men working in saw-pits, the remains of which can be seen frequently in the woods. Two men would operate a saw, one, the 'under-dog', often an apprentice, standing in the pit while the other, the 'top-dog', would guide the saw from above. The logs were then split by hand and the wood turned on simple lathes by the 'bodgers', who lived in the woods until they had produced a saleable load of legs and stretchers which would go to the factories in the towns or the village workshops.

Therefore beech was actively encouraged for the furniture trade and seeds and saplings were set to replace felled trees. However, over a long period of time the best trees were used and so those that remain today tend to be less healthy or poor specimens, which is one reason why these beautiful woods are under threat.

Ecology

Beech woods are very different from mixed woodland. The trees produce a dense shade and deep leaf litter so that the ground flora tends to be patchy, or in some places non-existent especially where the soil is very flinty and the ground is too dry. Shade-tolerant trees and shrubs like holly, yew and spurge laurel grow in some places while in others brambles cover the ground, few flowering in the deep shade. The smaller flowering plants are all those which flower in the spring before the leaf cover is too thick. Many of the ancient woodland indicator species mentioned above can be found especially in glades or along paths.

Two other plants to look out for which have evolved different methods of coping with the poor light conditions are dog's mercury and the well-known bluebell, a common sight in the beech woods. Dog's mercury flowers very early in the season with green flowers pollinated by insects. Plants are either male or female but also spread by underground stems or rhizomes. The leaves are present almost all year and persist in the driest summers, even though they may wilt, lasting to the end of the following winter. This strategy gives maximum efficiency in producing food by photosynthesis. Bluebells overcome the problem of shade by having a different life cycle. The bulbs sprout very early in the winter so that the plant can take advantage of the light afforded by the leafless conditions above. By the time the beech is fully in leaf, the bluebells have flowered, set seed and become dormant for the summer, the seeds germinating the following winter. Bluebells are not necessarily woodland plants but cannot tolerate much competition from vigorous grasses and plants or trampling from animals, so have taken refuge in a habitat which is not really adequate but which affords them some protection.

HEDGES

If woodland is cleared with a remnant left as a hedge, some of the woodland plants persist for many years, often for centuries. These species are not found in planted hedges, so act as a useful indication of the origin of the hedge. Many Chiltern hedges were formed from woodland relics and contrast with those to be seen down on the Oxfordshire plain which, although they may be several hundred years old with a number of shrub species present, were originally planted. The lack of woodland ground flora shows this.

CHALK GRASSLAND

History

It used to be thought that areas of open chalk grassland had never been covered with wildwood but more up-to-date evidence seems to show that woodland was present. Neolithic man, about four and a half thousand years ago, gradually started to clear the forest, the areas of chalk being easier to cultivate than heavy clay soil elsewhere. By the end of the Iron Age, two thousand years later, both arable cultivation and intensive sheep grazing were taking place on the chalk slopes. When agriculture became less intensive after the departure of the Romans, a proportion of the Chiltern grassland reverted to beech wood but other areas remained open and were used throughout the Middle Ages for sheep and cattle grazing.

By the seventeenth century the chalk downland of the Chilterns was being utilized for sheep–corn husbandry. The sheep, the Old Wiltshire or Western breed, were sturdy and agile, able to walk up and down the hills each day, and were famed for their ability to drop dung at night providing fertilizer for the arable fields at the foot of the scarp on which they were folded at night.

In times of agricultural expansion during the Napoleonic Wars and the mid-nineteenth century, chalk grassland was sometimes ploughed for arable land where the terrain allowed, but in the depressions which followed and which lasted to the Second World War, previously ploughed land was allowed to revert to grassland once more and in many cases was grazed only by rabbits. During the last war more grassland was ploughed but was not always cultivated; since then the main threats to chalk grassland have been the use of fertilizers to 'improve' the quantity of grass at the expense of flowering plants, and the myxomatosis epidemic which has reduced rabbit grazing and allowed the invasion of scrub.

Ecology

Chalk grassland is a semi-natural habitat, produced by the action of grazing which prevents the growth of scrub and woodland. It is characteristically rich in flowers which flourish owing to the lack of competition from tall grasses which cannot thrive when grazed or in poor soil and dry conditions.

Many plants show adaptations to cope with these conditions. Some, like salad burnet and lady's bedstraw, have very long root systems, advantageous when the top soil dries out. Others, often members of the daisy family, conserve water by having hairy leaves or by pressing their leaves close to the ground, often forming a rosette: adaptations which at the same time reduce the effects of grazing. Plants belonging to the legume or pea family, like vetches and bird's foot trefoil, fix nitrogen from the air, so improving their nutrition.

Today chalk grassland is managed by careful sheep grazing to retain this mixture of flowers and this goes hand in hand with maintaining an associated rich variety of animals and insects, conspicuous amongst which are butterflies and moths.

Anthills, made by colonies of yellow ants, are a feature of old grassland and show by their size how long the grassland has remained undisturbed. The soil particles are small and after a time the orginal flora is buried. A characteristic plant community develops with such plants as forget-me-not and wall speedwell, annuals which produce many seeds to recolonize during the next season, while thyme and rock rose are perennials which can tolerate burial as the ants build up the mound.

The Past in the Landscape

In the area covered by this series of walks there is a contrast between the landscape on the Oxfordshire plain and that on the Chiltern hills themselves. This contrast is historically the result of the different topography and geology in the two areas which in the past led to variation in the development of agricultural methods and patterns of settlement.

THE MIDDLE AGES

On the rich fertile soil of the Oxfordshire plain along the foot of the Chiltern escarpment, settlements grew up along the spring line and the land was cleared of woodland many centuries ago.

By the early Middle Ages, each village had some form of open field farming with two or three huge fields, divided into furlongs which were further subdivided into strips, held by tenants. Each individual held land scattered throughout the fields, so sharing good or poor conditions. Crops were grown in a two- or three-year rotation, details differing from place to place, so each year one field would lie fallow or unsown to allow the soil to rest and to get rid of weeds. The fallow field would provide grazing for animals as would the other fields after harvest. The land was ploughed in such a way as to produce high ridges of soil from which water would drain into the dividing furrows. In the fourteenth century some arable land was laid down to pasture after the reduction in the work force due to the Black Death and these ridges and furrows were grassed over and still remain visible in some places.

Permanent hay meadows, near water for the best crop, were also grazed for certain months of the year. Villages like Cuxham, away from the foot of the escarpment, had small areas of commonland or waste, which provided more grazing and also fuel in the form of wood or scrub. However the villages along the foot of the hills had the best of both worlds as their territory included not only the fertile plain but also the scarp and the hilltop beyond. Common land was often on the scarp as in Crowell or Shirburn, while other larger manors like Aston Rowant or Pyrton had common land which extended for several miles beyond the top of the hills. Obviously these villages had no shortage of grazing or of timber resources and often came to an agreement with other less well endowed manors who could then share in these assets as did Cuxham and Pyrton.

In the hills themselves, the wooded and heathy terrain led to the formation of a different agricultural landscape. People lived in isolated hamlets, their fields carved out of the woodland over the years, a process called 'assarting'. Instead of large open fields, these were smaller, more numerous and enclosed by hedges formed from remnants of woodland. Some of these fields were farmed in common by tenants, and crops were rotated in a similar way to that on the plain while other fields were owned either by the lord of the manor or by individual farmers. Sheep were important and were kept in large numbers.

The woodland was an important asset to the local people. In the Middle Ages it was a mixture of tall timber trees and coppiced underwood, which was managed by periodic cutting to provide a continuous supply of wood for fuel, fencing and poles. This was more important than mature timber and because of ready access to London via the River Thames, this was a thriving industry until the eighteenth century. Some woodland was in private ownership and was separated by ditches and banks from that used for common land, where tenants and villagers had rights to graze their livestock, cut wood for fuel and repairs and right of pannage, when pigs were allowed to feed on fallen beech mast and acorns. The composition of the woodland was more mixed than now with oak, ash, elm and hazel as well as beech, which even then seems to have been the predominant species.

ENCLOSURES

By Tudor times (sixteenth century) some tenants in the open fields were beginning to amalgamate their strips to make cultivation easier and gradually this move away from the open field system was seen to be a more efficient way to farm. New legume and fodder crops and better rotation improved the soil quality so that by the mid-eighteenth century major landowners were imposing a new system of smaller, regular shaped, hedged fields on their land. New farms were built, often away from the village, roads were realigned and the old common land was turned into agricultural land. This led to a social upheaval in many places where the smallholders lost their land in the reorganization and became labourers on the large farms. At first this enclosure was organized by agreement of all concerned, later by Private Acts of Parliament for particular parishes. By the time enclosure came to many of the villages in our area, there was a General Enclosure Act which contained more safeguards for the poor such as the provision of allotments to mitigate the effect of the loss of common land.

At the foot of the Chiltern escarpment, the open field system worked well on the rich fertile soil, producing good crop yields so the landscape remained unchanged until well into the nineteenth century. Enclosure transformed the wide open vistas with few hedges into neat, ordered countryside with miles of new hawthorn hedges planted at the landowners' expense to make the new fields. Since the Second World War many of these hedges have been grubbed up to allow easy access to large modern machinery, the landscape changing yet again with public outcry, this time from conservationists.

Enclosure also made a change in the Chiltern hills although not to such an extent. Most of the fields had always been enclosed so the major effect was on the large areas of common land which were mostly enclosed under the General Acts in the mid to late nineteenth century. In some places common land still exists such as at Russell's Water, although with an altered appearance from the scrubby heath of the past.

ROADS AND TRACKS

The Icknield Way

This is reputed to be one of the oldest routes in England: at least 4000 years old. It originally linked Wessex and East Anglia and took its name from a later tribe, the Iceni, to whose territory it led. Originally it was not a marked track but a wide belt of transit up to a mile (2 km) in width which mostly kept to the fairly well drained Lower chalk at the base of the hills.

In the intervening centuries it has gradually been narrowed and formalized by settlement and agriculture; the Romans improved some of the track along what is now the Lower Icknield Way. Some of the walks in this guide use the remains of this wide belt which is now three parallel routes that can clearly be seen on an OS map. The Upper and Lower Icknield Ways were used as drove roads up to the nineteenth century when the Enclosure Awards reduced them to bridleways. The Upper Icknield Way is still a long-distance path, now for recreation rather than for communication, and takes its modern name, the Ridgeway, from the section along the top of the Berkshire Downs. The third track, the Chiltern Ridgeway, was used as an alternative summer route when the clay soil was dry enough for easy travel. It can still be traced today, both as a footpath and as a road.

Other routes

Many of the paths, tracks and green lanes followed along our trails are centuries old and their origins are lost in the mists of time. Some follow the paths which would have crossed the open fields, losing importance only after the Parliamentary Enclosures, while others link outlying hamlets with the parish church as at Pishill or Aston Rowant. Many, especially on the Chiltern escarpment, led between different areas within parishes to utilize various resources such as timber on the slopes and common grazing land on the plateau. Some survive as deep holloways which may also have been followed by packhorses and waggons, with sleds being used for transport in the steepest places. As some roads were improved, so other, once important, routes fell into obscurity. Knightsbridge Lane which travels the length of Pyrton parish and on down towards Henley is a good example, now surviving as no more than a farm lane in many places.

Other roads remain important but their route has changed over the centuries. The present A40 down Aston Hill has followed this route only since 1824; previously it took a different course downhill and in the Middle Ages was an important *via regis* or King's road. It was known even then as London Weye. In 1718 it came under the care of a Turnpike Trust which widened and surfaced roads to improve them from the generally appalling earlier conditions. This old route is now possibly the best surfaced bridleway in the county!

In the landscape the age of a track can be guessed by its shape: the older ones which evolved through the passage of time usually have steep-sided banks and follow a winding course; the more modern straight enclosure roads, laid out no more than 150 to 200 years ago, have characteristically wide grass verges which were left to allow for the passage of herds of animals and to compensate for the poor conditions before the advent of a proper surface.

BOUNDARIES

Within the landscape, clues can be found to boundaries between parishes and different types of land-use. Many parishes are thought to date from Iron Age or Roman times and some have Anglo-Saxon boundary charters, the earliest written evidence, still in existence. Parishes along the Chiltern escarpment have a characteristic long narrow shape, taking in land on the plain which was suitable for cultivation, the settlement on the spring line for water, the scarp itself and land on the plateau with its woodland and rough heath for timber and firewood, as well as further grazing. Usually the boundary has remained unchanged since then and in places can be marked by an old hedge or a bank. With the help of an Ordnance Survey map on which present-day boundaries are marked it is interesting to see how often this occurs. Good examples of old parish boundary banks can be seen on the Crowell and Christmas Common trails. Banks in woodland can mark the line of an old ownership or management, or sometimes the former edge of the woodland itself, now lost because of later planting as in Halfridge Wood at Bix.

PLACE NAMES

This is a vast subject, full of pitfalls for the non-expert. However, it is interesting to relate some elements in place names to the landscape which was described by the early inhabitants of the area. Some names incorporate words which indicate the presence of water, like 'burna', a stream, as at Shirburn, or 'well', a spring, as at Crowell. Both these settlements are on the springline at the foot of the Chilterns. Other names describe the setting of the settlement like a valley or a clearing in woodland. The Anglo-Saxons had several words for different types of valleys. 'Denu' means a main valley as at Assendon while 'cumb' marks a shorter valley like the one at Swyncombe. Another word 'ora' occurs for the foot of a slope and is found in names like Stonor and Lewknor. In the Chilterns with its long woodland history names are to be found which reflect this. Names ending in 'ley' have their root in the Old English word for a clearing or a glade although the earliest meaning is wood or forest as at Henley: high wood. Sometimes individual trees have left their mark as place names; Bix comes from the word for box tree and Pyrton is named after a pear orchard. These are just a few examples of descriptive place names in the area of these trails. Look out for more as you follow the maps.

Sanicle

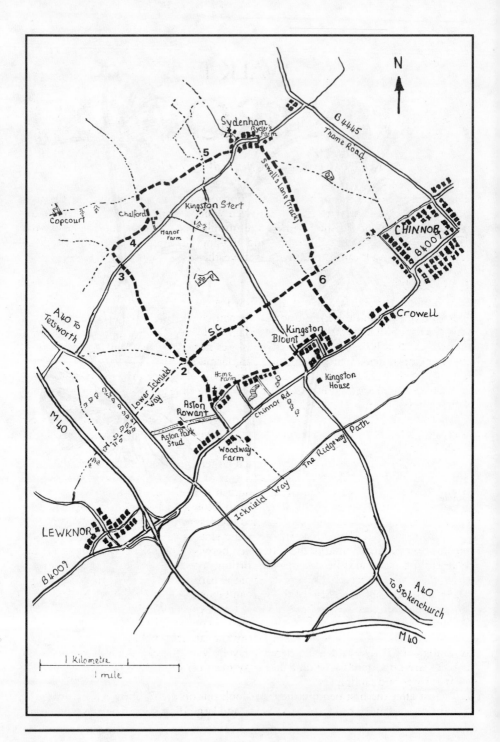

N

Sydenham
Ryder's Farm
B4445 Thame Road
5
Kingston Stert
Sewell's Lane (Track)
Copcourt
Chalford
Manor Farm
4
CHINNOR
B4007
3
6
A40 To Tetsworth
S.C.
Crowell
Kingston Blount
2
Lower Icknield Way
Home Farm
Kingston House
M40
Aston Rowant
Chinnor Rd.
Aston Park Stud.
Woodway Farm
The Ridgeway Path
Icknield Way
LEWKNOR
B4009
A40 To Stokenchurch
M40

1 Kilometre
1 mile

WALK 1

ASTON ROWANT

6 miles (10 km), or shorter walk of 5 miles (8 km)

This is a level walk through the lower portions of Aston Rowant and Crowell parishes via Sydenham. This and the Crowell Walk (2) show the two elements of the Chiltern escarpment parishes; namely the up-hill wooded areas and the below-hill springline villages with rich arable land making the most of the available local resources. The walk can be muddy in wet weather.

1 SU728990

Start near the eleventh-century church of St Peter and Paul in Aston Rowant. Walk past a box hedge and the main door of the church. If the church is open, go in and look for the old map which shows the village and its surroundings in the eighteenth century. You will see the small fields or closes near the village and also part of the two huge open fields which were still being farmed in strips.

Outside, notice the plants like wall rue fern colonizing the church wall. Many churchyards have been undisturbed for a very long time and so have developed into valuable wildlife areas.

The path leads down some steps to the road where the trail turns right past some cottages. After a time the tarred surface gives way to a stony track which can be flooded after rain.

Aston Rowant was originally a much larger parish and included what is now Stokenchurch. It was likely to have been part of an important Saxon royal estate, being the East Tun (settlement) to distinguish it from the West Tun (now South Weston) and the King's Tun (now Kingston Blount). The other part of the name comes from the Rohan family who owned the manor later.

As you walk, notice the stream at the side of the track. The presence of a plentiful water supply marks the difference between this area of the parish on the Oxfordshire plain and the dry up-hill portion, a feature shared by many parishes along the Chiltern escarpment. This part of the parish is below the spring line, where water seeps through the chalk of the hills and emerges at the point where it meets a band of more impervious rock, in this case lower greensand. Further along the trail, the underlying geology changes again to gault clay around the Chalford area where the water-table is only a few inches below the surface, making the ground easily waterlogged. The stream is bordered by yellow flag and pendulous sedge. Such habitats are important to wildlife and may even occasionally be visited by waders such as snipe and sandpipers.

Just after the first bend in the track look out on the right for a special type of hawthorn with much more rounded leaves and larger flowers and berries than usual.

These few bushes are examples of midland hawthorn which usually grows only in old woodland or where woodland has been cleared leaving a remnant to form a hedge.

2 SU723994

The track meets the Lower Icknield Way, an old medieval drove road parallel to today's Icknield Way or Ridgeway. It was originally part of the prehistoric Icknield Way and was later possibly the route used and improved by the Romans (see Introduction). At this point there is a wet patch on the left where you can find fool's water cress, meadow sweet and comfrey, the latter much used as a herbal remedy to aid healing injuries and infections.

The trail bears left for a short distance before heading to the right, past a line of pollarded willows following the line of a stream, along a good track over the fields. As you cross the wide expanse of arable field, there is a panorama behind of the Chiltern escarpment topped by the landmark of the telecommunications tower at Stokenchurch visible for miles around.

This track is an old one called Copcourt Church Way, linking the hamlet of Copcourt with the parish church of Aston Rowant. Although the bird population in arable fields has dropped in recent years there are still skylarks to be seen or heard as you cross the field. There are also some arable weeds along the edge of the path, look for cut-leaved geranium with rounded, very divided leaves and small pink flowers. A strip of woodland has recently been planted and this provides a refuge for wildlife, especially pheasant, partridge and rabbits. Some willows here are female trees, their spikey catkins, differing from the silky male pussy willow, will later produce masses of cottony seeds.

3 SP716005

When the road is reached cross straight over and continue down the track. Here the landscape changes from the large open fields to smaller enclosed ones which have looked like this for centuries. The fields crossed earlier traditionally grew corn and were famed in the nineteenth century for their fertility whereas these smaller fields around Copcourt, over the hill to the left, and Chalford to the right, were dairy farms, utilizing the plentiful supply of water and the lush grass and hay. There are signs of ridge-and-furrow in a field ahead which show that it was put down to pasture during the Middle Ages and has not been ploughed since.

Just before the pine and poplar plantation turn right over the stile and follow the edge of the field. In spring, poplars are sometimes attacked by groups of small black beetle larvae which chew away patches of soft tissue between the leaf veins, leaving brown skeletonized areas. The adult beetles in summer are shiny metallic blue and green, hence their common-name of jewel beetles.

A few small oak trees along the edge of the plantation bear various galls on their twigs and leaves, all caused by larvae of members of the wasp family. Hard round brown marble-sized galls are oak marbles formed from damaged leaf buds. On the underside of the leaves may be large numbers of small flattened circular galls known as spangle galls. A third type is the irregularly shaped knopper gall on acorns, caused by a recently introduced pest.

Church of St Peter and Paul

Sewell Lane, Sydenham

Fungus on tree stump

4 SP719008

Go through the gate at the far end. Cross the track and go over the fence opposite. Continue along the left-hand field edge through two gates. When a gravel drive is reached, cross over and take a narrow path alongside a fence overhung by a white poplar tree. Climb over the stile, almost hidden in the trees, and in the field turn left and follow the line of an old hedge on the edge of a deep drainage ditch. Through the hedge you can see bumps and hollows in the grass. This was the site of the village of Chalford which is now no more than two farms and some cottages. A local story says that the plague was brought here from Norfolk in 1582, which may have been a factor in the decline of this settlement.

The trail follows the hedge, turning left on to a concrete drive at Manor Farm where there was once a water mill. Follow the track beside a stream for a while. Both ditches and streams provide good habitats for moisture-loving plants such as brooklime with blue flowers, water mint and water forget-me-not.

Turn right over a stile beside an electricity pylon. Cross the field making for the right-hand corner where a stile crosses the hedge. Continue over the next field to a grassy track heading slightly right towards a thatched cottage in the distance. At an old barn keep straight on with the hedge and cottage to the right. Look at the grassy fields over the hedge and on the slope to the left. They all show ridge-and-furrow which is most obvious in the late spring when the ridges are covered with buttercups which prefer the drier conditions there. Sometimes the ridges continue in the same direction through several present day fields, showing the extent of the large medieval fields. The hedge on your immediate right contains many shrub species and this can indicate its age if the species in a thirty yard stretch are counted. An approximate age can be said to be equal to one hundred years for each shrub species counted.

5 SP726015

After crossing a stile and small bridge over a ditch, the trail leads over ridge-and-furrow to a stile on to a green lane. Cross the lane and walk through the allotment gardens and then through a narrow field on to the road where you turn left.

The name Sydenham means the place at the wide river meadow and in the Domesday Book this was a notable feature of the manor, which was recorded with sixty acres of meadow, an unusually large amount in this area. The village, which had a long connection with Thame Abbey, used to be slightly larger; near the church and to the north of the village traces of earthworks can be seen: all that remains of small medieval cottages and their yards.

In the village head past The Crown on the right and the church, with an unusual nineteenth-century wooden tower, on the left and continue along the main road until a track on the right marked 'No through road' is reached opposite Ryder's Farm. Take this track which continues for some distance. This is Sewell Lane or Mill Way and was used by Crowell villagers to get to the mill at Sydenham. Another name for the track is Hollier's Lane and it is thought that it linked with Collier's Lane (Crowell trail, Walk 2) as a cross-country drove route to the cattle market at Thame.

In autumn parts of the hedgerows are richly decorated with red rose hips and fruits of woody nightshade, blackberries and ivy flowers; all good food for birds, mice and insects. On damp dewy autumn days the hedgerow plants are festooned with spiders' webs. Compare the fine round orb webs in open areas with flat sheet webs in dense vegetation.

As you pass through a tunnel formed by over-hanging elderberry bushes it is possible to see clearly the original width of the track, which is obscured further back. The path crosses a bridge over a small marshy area and carries straight on to rejoin the Lower Icknield Way.

6 SP739004

The trail turns right along the track.

SHORT CUT Follow the track back to Aston Rowant, emerging at point 2 where you turn left and retrace your steps back to the church.

After a short distance another track goes off to the left which leads to Crowell. Follow this and as you walk look at the Chiltern escarpment ahead and see if you can pick out areas to the left which appear to be different to the main cover of beechwoods. These patches are likely to have been common land where Crowell tenants with common rights could cut underwood. Since these rights were lost when Crowell was enclosed in 1882, the woodland has regenerated with more varied species in contrast to the managed beechwoods on either side, hence the different colour of the vegetation when seen from a distance. These can be explored on the Crowell trail (Walk 2). Further to the right along the escarpment tenants in Kingston Blount had rights to 'hillwerk', a local name for common rights on the wooded escarpment. Tenants with five acres of land were entitled to half a load of small wood for fuel and repairs every two years. By the eighteenth century this was for the poor only and by 1832 the area used was called Poor's Hillock. The rights were extinguished in 1864 and the poor common was purchased in exchange for four acres of allotment gardens which can still be seen further along the trail.

At the road turn right for 500 yards. Walk with care as the road is busy. At Kingston Blount turn right down Pleck Lane. At Brook Street turn left and look out for the allotments, Hillock Gardens, on the right. Go straight across the minor road and continue along the path back to Aston Rowant. Follow the path past the small village school and along the edge of a green, past Home Farm back to the start.

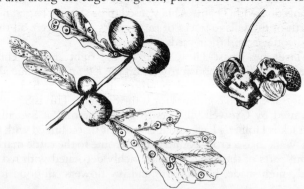

Oak galls

Elder avenue

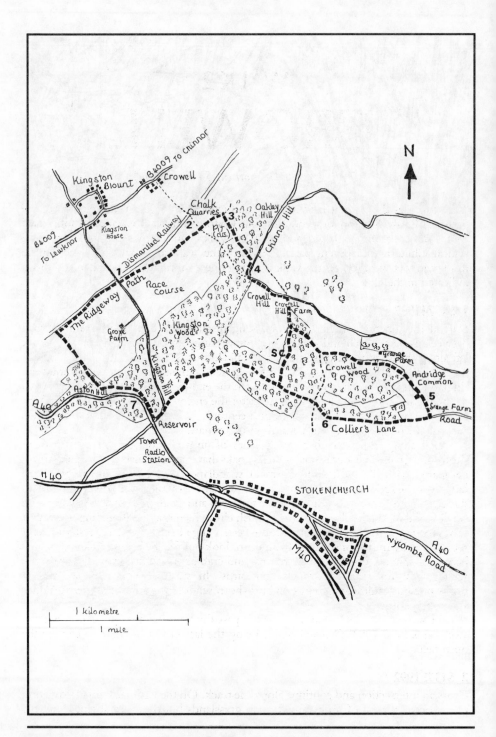

WALK 2

CROWELL

7 miles (11 km), short cut 5 miles (8 km)

This trail uses the ancient Icknield Way and explores the old up-hill portion of the parish of Crowell before descending to the Oxfordshire plain via another long-used route. Its landscape contrasts with that of Walk 1 and shows the two parts of a typical Chiltern escarpment parish. Parts of the walk are quite steep and can be muddy in wet weather. As the walk is a long one a short cut can be taken and this is indicated in the text.

1 SU741987

Start at the junction of the Ridgeway long distance footpath and the minor road between Stokenchurch and Kingston Blount (Kingston Hill). Facing the hills, walk left along the track towards some distant tall chimneys.

The broad grassy track is the Icknield Way, an ancient route across southern England linking Wessex and East Anglia. In the eighteenth century it was still a well defined road but became less important after the enclosure of the open fields and the formation of new roads in the nineteenth century. The width of the track reflects its past use for the passage of large numbers of animals.

All along its length there are patches of unspoilt flora and many species of shrub and tree. The occasional solitary oaks have an expansive, spreading form compared with the tall spindly form of woodland oaks. Notice the shape of the hawthorn hedge cut with an angled top which encourages the lower growth to thicken, so improving its wildlife value for birds and small mammals. As you pass a small wood on the left look out for English elm which may be flowering in May. It produces large clusters of oval yellow-green winged seeds which are sterile, as it reproduces by means of suckers. In autumn, look out for the bright pink and orange berries of spindle, often eaten by robins, and crab apples which provide a welcome winter feast for small mammals and birds. In summer you may see yellow brimstone butterflies laying eggs on buckthorn whose insignificant flowers produce an exotic perfume.

The fields on each side of the track past the woodland were farmed as open strip fields until 1882, Crowell parish being the last in Oxfordshire to enclose the open fields.

2 SU751992

Cross an intersection and continue along the track. On the left many small flowering plants occur typical of undisturbed chalk grasslands but these are absent along the cultivated field edge. The hedgerow contains a succession of flowering shrubs including field maple and buckthorn in late spring and dog rose and wild clematis or traveller's joy in early summer. The clematis thrives in chalky soil and later in the year transforms the hedgerow with clouds of fluffy grey seed heads which give rise to its other name of old man's beard.

Through the hedge on the left you can glimpse water-filled quarries remaining after chalk extraction for the cement works at Chinnor which have been in operation since 1908.

3 SU754994

Take the public footpath to the right amongst trees and follow it uphill. As you climb look at the varied trees growing here unlike the typical beech woods which will be seen later on. You will see much sycamore with yew and silvery-leaved whitebeam. Many of the trees along the path have short trunks with branches spreading from a low level. This shows that they have been cut or coppiced at some time in the past when this area was used as common land by the people of Crowell who had rights to cut underwood (see Aston Rowant, Walk 1).

After a steep climb look out on the left for a bank running parallel to the path which marks the boundary between Crowell and Chinnor parishes. A contrast in the tree cover can be seen with tall timber trees on the Chinnor side and coppiced beech in Crowell, reflecting their different management in the past.

As the path reaches the top of the hill you will notice oak trees appearing as the soil changes to clay-with-flints. Oaks do not thrive on the chalky soil of the escarpment. Another feature of old common land can also be seen here; the rough pits and hollows are the remains of diggings for clay for pottery and bricks as often commoners had 'mineral' rights on common land utilizing whatever the local geology provided.

4 SU757989

Keep the fence of a house on your left until you reach a road. Turn right and continue along the road for some distance.

In early spring a strong garlic smell with reveal large clumps of ransoms growing just inside the woodland edge on the right. The track joining the road from the right on the bend used to link the main village of Crowell with this up-hill hamlet.

The road starts to descend and opposite a house on the left called Rushes turn right down a concrete drive signed Crowell Hill Farm. After twenty yards turn left down a holloway. Keep to the left at a junction of paths.

SHORT CUT At the junction take the centre path which keeps the woodland edge on the right for a distance. Continue until you descend onto a path running up a valley turning right to rejoin the main trail as described at point 6.

Parallel to the path is another boundary bank and ditch, this time between the parishes of Crowell and Radnage to the left. This line also marks the Hundred boundary between Lewknor and Desborough as well as the Oxfordshire and

Whitebeam leaves

Pinkish Sickener

Penny Bun

Townhall Clock

Buckinghamshire county boundary. In the Middle Ages Radnage was included in the Royal Manor of Brill which was part of the Royal Forest of Bernwood and was possibly included in the area of the King's hunting forest. Thus there are several reasons why the banks along this stretch are still so distinct as they were very important in the past.

Look for plants which show by their names their strong association with ancient woodland such as wood melick grass, woodruff and wood sorrel. These plants die back by late summer but in autumn a rich variety of fungi takes their place. Many are well camouflaged in the fallen leaves but it is interesting to see how many different species occur. Two different types which can be found are the spongy brown caps of penny bun *(Boletus)* which have pores on the underside and the pinkish sickener *(Russula)* which has gills and is poisonous.

The path finally comes into the open near Grange Farm which used to be called Bottom Farm. The hillside to the left is covered with cowslips and blue speedwell in the spring and was originally part of Andridge Common, one of two Radnage commons.

The path bears right and becomes a track leading past arable fields and agricultural buildings.

5 SU777972

Follow the track to a junction and turn right along another old route known as Collier's Lane. The name comes from the industry of charcoal making which took place in the woods, but the road was likely to have been used as a drove road avoiding tolls on the turnpike (now the A40) and linking eventually with Thame and the market there (see Walk 1). The track not only follows the parish boundary between Crowell and Stokenchurch on the left but again marks the county boundary between Oxfordshire and Buckinghamshire; until 1896 Stokenchurch was part of Oxfordshire and some local residents still regret the change! The track heads up the valley with the landmark of the Stokenchurch telecommunications tower on the skyline. At a junction the trail turns right and soon enters the wood.

6 SU765974

The path continues straight on with the field visible on the left through the trees. The short cut rejoins the main trail along this section of the walk.

In the spring the flora is rich with bluebells, violets, yellow archangel and woodruff with tiny white star-shaped flowers and vanilla scented leaves which are arranged like a collar round the stem.

As the track travels deeper into the woods its age becomes more apparent, with flinty banks on each side, covered with moss encouraged by the cool damp conditions and absence of leaf litter. Another fungus to look out for here in the autumn is yellow sulphur tuft, usually growing on dead stumps.

At a junction of tracks Collier's Lane keeps to the left along the woodland edge. When it reaches the top of the hill it bears left, being joined by another track.

At this point the trail is following a prehistoric ridgeway, used when the going was dry as an alternative summer route to the Icknield Way. In winter this clay surface would have been unusable for much traffic, hence the formation of the broad track lower down on the chalky, well drained surface of the lower slopes of the escarpment (see Introduction).

After a short distance the trail reaches a cottage and the road. Turn left along the road but walk with care as traffic is fast here. At the junction with the A40 turn right for a short time.

7 SU745974

Turn right down a bridleway, the old coach road, leading off the main road marked by a National Trust sign. Follow this downhill.

This track was originally the main route westwards from London to Oxford and beyond and was one of the medieval *via regis* or King's roads. It was turnpiked in 1718, hence its good surface, but the route to Oxford was altered in 1824 to the line of the present A40. A deep holloway, an even older route, runs downhill to the right hidden in the trees and can be seen further along the walk.

Several interesting plants grow along the track including wild gooseberry and moscatel or townhall clock, so named because the flowerhead faces in four directions.

Continue downhill until a steep bridleway leads down to the right over steps in a chalk bank. This leads into a sunken path, called Wood Way which linked Aston Rowant and Stokenchurch via the holloway which can now be seen partly hidden by vegetation. These two settlements were originally part of the same parish, Aston Rowant. The rich arable soil was cultivated on the plain while the woodland and rough ground on the hills around Stokenchurch provided commonland, grazing, minerals and carefully managed timber resources. In this area look for the shiny-leaved spurge laurel which bears a slight resemblance to garden laurel, but in fact is not related to either laurel or spurge. This plant is another which indicates old woodland.

Wood Way leaves the woodland and crosses arable fields between hedges. These fields were part of the Upper Field, one of Aston Rowant's two huge open fields which were enclosed in 1832. The crops produced in this area were of high quality which is one reason why there was little pressure to change the farming system by enclosure, the open fields remaining in use in this area until relatively late.

8 SU734981

The path now reaches the Ridgeway once more and the trail turns right. Running close to the track is the route of the dismantled railway which was opened in 1872 with a station at Aston Rowant. The line was closed in 1957.

There is a clear view of the escarpment from here with the bulk of Aston Hill and Kingston Hill. In the Civil War this area was a boundary between Royalist and Parliamentarian forces with, in July 1643, a great body of the King's Horse camping under these hills and a Parliamentarian garrison not far away at Thame.

Look out for hornbeam hedges and trees, at first glance they could be mistaken for beech, but the leaves have a folded appearance and coarser texture and the branches tend to be twisted. The timber is very hard and was used for cogs and wooden screws. After about half a mile (1 km) the starting point is reached.

Spurge Laurel

Dryad saddle fungus

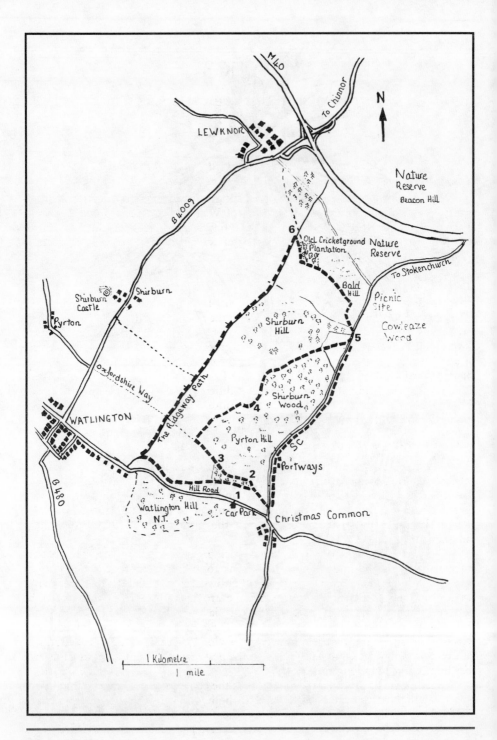

WALK 3

SHIRBURN

6.75 miles (10.5 km), short cut 4 miles (6.5 km)

This trail is mostly in the open areas of chalk grassland, the remnants of the sheep-grazing land of the springline settlements of Watlington, Shirburn and Lewknor. Parts are steep and can be slippery and the return along the Icknield Way can be muddy in places in wet weather. If a shorter walk is desired take the short cut at point 5.

1 SU710935

Start from the car park for the National Trust land at the top of Watlington Hill. Turn right out of the car park and walk along the road to the junction. Turn left here and after fifty yards take the path to the left over a stile and along a hedge. This field looks pink in the summer because of the flowerheads of Yorkshire fog, a soft velvety grass. Buttercups and ox-eye daisies add to the colourful effect in June.

Climb a stile and bear right across the field in front of the hawthorn bushes. The grass at the field edge near the scrub is different from that in the first field as it has not been 'improved' and hence many more flowering plants are to be found, though grazing keeps them small.

2 SU713938

The path leads over another stile and downhill along an old track. This track is part of Knightsbridge Lane which runs the length of Pyrton parish and which you will come across again in the walks at Cuxham and Christmas Common. Here it is also part of the Oxfordshire Way. As you emerge into the open you can see Knightsbridge Lane stretching ahead into the distance north to Pyrton village and beyond.

The grassland here is full of plants which grow on chalk. Some, like stemless thistle, have ground-hugging growth forms to avoid grazing since this type of grassland is only maintained by grazing either by sheep or rabbits. Other species like thyme, and the taller basil and marjoram have strong-tasting leaves which tend to be left by animals (but used by humans for flavouring in cooking). Notice the hummocks of anthills, many quite large. These are a sign of long undisturbed pastureland and can be seen in many places along this trail (see Introduction). In autumn you may see large 'fairy rings' in the grass, another indication that this area has been stable for a long time.

Across the grassy valley to the right are the contrasting colours of different tree species with the dark evergreen yew and the lighter foliage of groups of silver birch. Both these species tend to be amongst the first to appear when woodland is developing on chalky soil, the seeds being spread easily, by birds in the case of yew and those of silver birch by the wind.

Much of the grassland along this walk is being invaded by shrubs such as hawthorn, rose, buckthorn, dogwood and privet. All these bear berries and the seeds are spread by birds and animals eating the berries for food. Bird species have preferences for different berries; blackbirds like hawthorn, starlings, song thrushes and redwings favour dogwood. The black glossy fruits of privet are clustered at the end of the flexible stems and are therefore difficult to eat. They are not very nutritious and tend to be left to later in the winter when they are eaten by blackbirds and bullfinches.

3 SU706943

Continue downhill past a house and woodyard on the left, a reminder of the traditional Chiltern timber industry, until a grassy path goes off to the right. Take this path which follows the line of the escarpment and passes between areas of grassland and scrub.

In spring cowslips flower here on the short turf, followed later in the year by the purple clustered bellflower and white candytuft, a local speciality which favours bare patches like rabbit scrapes. Look out for carline thistle which has golden seedheads.

As you walk, notice how the scrub is taking over the grassland in places and how in others a coarse green-yellow grass is becoming dominant, replacing the finer grasses and flowers. This is because the grazing pressure has gone since the removal of sheep and the drop in the rabbit population. Much of the Chiltern escarpment in this area was common land used for sheep grazing by the inhabitants of the villages on the spring line below. In 1835 this Pyrton Hill had 170 acres of sheep common with twenty-two acres for cows, but when the land changed to private ownership after the Parliamentary Enclosure in 1851, common grazing would have ceased. Later agricultural depressions and changes in farming techniques meant that gradually the use of this land changed and so scrub and woodland like the yew wood on your right developed on the herb-rich downs.

Keep on the path as it follows the edge of woodland. In the winter a holloway can be seen through the yew trees to the right of the path. This is the route of an older track probably used for driving sheep to and from the grazing land where they fed on the grassland by day, at night returning to the village where they were folded on the fields, their dung providing fertilizer.

4 SU715950

Follow the path along the edge of Shirburn Wood with a wire fence on the left. The woodland varies along the path, some being predominantly beech managed over the years for timber production while in other places it appears to be more mixed, perhaps the result of less selective felling. Look out for magpie inkcap toadstool here in the autumn, named because of its white and black colouration.

The path eventually emerges into the open at the bottom of the steep slope of Shirburn Hill. Notice as you climb, how different this grassland is to that of Pyrton

Redwing

Candytuft

Carline Thistle

Magpie Inkcap

Hill. The grazing by rabbits is more intense here and the predominant flora varies from time to time as a result. You may find yellow ragwort or white wild candytuft most noticeable but smaller plants can also be found, such as stonecrop on the bare soil or the diminutive pale pink flowers of squinancywort, whose odd name comes from the medieval Latin word for quinsy, a disease which this plant was thought to cure.

In midsummer groups of orange and black striped cinnabar moth caterpillars feed on the poisonous ragwort and the bright red and black adult moths can be seen as they fly by day. The bright colours of this species act as a warning to bird or animal predators; both larvae and moths are unpleasant to eat as they contain poisonous compounds gained from their ragwort food.

Look back to see the view over the fields below. The old names of these nearby fields show their history; Scrubfurlong was part of the medieval open field formed by the clearance of scrub for arable land, while Lynhull and Flax Hill were used for the cultivation of flax for linen. Old documents record the South Field, one of Shirburn's large open fields as stretching as far as 'le doune' or the down, a reference to the use of these hills for sheep.

The path climbs through a woodland edge, then crosses a stile and leads diagonally right across a field to a stile onto the road.

5 SU724954

SHORT CUT Turn right here and return to the start along the road which is a continuation of the prehistoric summer ridgeway mentioned in the Crowell trail, Walk 2.

Turn left along the road for a short distance, then left down a path signed Lewknor near an information board about the Aston Rowant National Nature Reserve. Follow the path downhill through hawthorn trees until it comes out at the top of a dry valley which used to be called Lewknor Warren. The patch of elderberry bushes here is a sure indicator of the presence of rabbits as it is a shrub whose bark they dislike. Consequently groups of elder often grow around the burrows and show past or present rabbit activity.

The path turns right along a wire fence marking the boundary of the Nature Reserve. There is no public access here but on the far side of the M40 there is an interpretive centre and nature trail with guide books available.

Looking over the fence colourful species-rich chalk grassland can be seen with, in late summer, the purple flowers of the autumn gentians. Amongst the grasses the easiest to identify is quaking grass, named for its large flower heads which nod in the wind. Meadow brown, marbled white, common blue and triangular shaped fast-flying skipper butterflies fly over the area in the summer. Butterflies prefer longer grassland like this because it provides food for caterpillars in contrast to the short, cropped grassland seen earlier which tends to support fewer more specialized species. The grassland here is managed by periodic sheep grazing and scrub clearance to prevent it becoming overgrown with hawthorn and dogwood.

Continue along the path, over a stile until a path leads off to the right through a copse known as Old Cricketground Plantation after the story that it was won by the Shirburn estate as a result of a wager on a local cricket match.

Crossing a short stretch of field you are aware of the M40 motorway which was opened here in 1973. Its route bisects the Aston Rowant Nature Reserve and has had a detrimental effect on the surroundings because of the noise caused by the ever-increasing volume of traffic on the concrete road surface.

6 SU718965

Turn left along the wide grassy track of the Ridgeway (see Walks 1 and 2 and Introduction). The track is followed for just over a mile (2 km), first bordered with hedges and more flowers which like chalky soil such as knapweed, field scabious and the yellow agrimony. These flowers provide a good source of nectar for different species of bumblebees whose names reflect their varying colour patterns; red-tailed, white-tailed and buff bumblebees.

Further on, the track winds through areas of woodland and thick hedges with the occasional glimpse of the escarpment followed earlier in the walk. See how the ground flora in these places changes to a woodland type with such species as dog's mercury. In winter you can see that many of the trees in the hedgerow have been coppiced in the past.

After crossing the intersection with the Oxfordshire Way marked by a wooden sign post, the hedges to the right become lower and in late autumn are swathed with the poisonous red berries of black bryony, a showy replacement for the insignificant greenish flowers earlier in the year.

After about half a mile (1 km) take a narrow footpath off to the left which climbs through trees and bushes, following the line of a deep holloway, overgrown with privet. You will also see the occasional sharp-leaved juniper, the rarest of our three native conifers, the others being yew and scots pine.

The path gradually climbs through more open grassland with numerous shrubs and flowers as described earlier in the walk in section 2. The line of the path and holloway indicates the line of an earlier route to Christmas Common from Watlington and is shown as such on an old map dated 1797. Continue uphill until you reach the stile crossed early in the trail. Follow the field edge back to the road and return to your starting point.

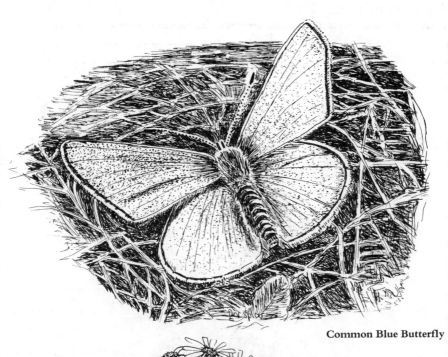

Common Blue Butterfly

Cinnabar Moth caterpillars feeding on Ragwort

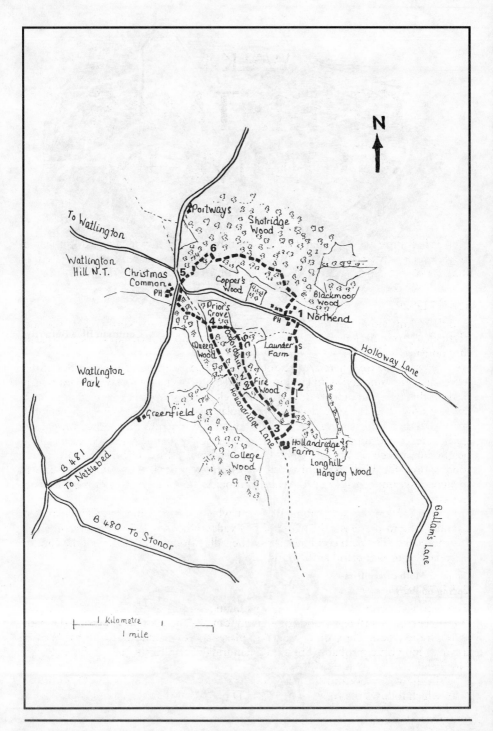

N

To Watlington

Portways
Shotridge
Wood

6

Watlington
Hill N.T.
5
Christmas
Common
PH

Copper's
Wood

Blackmoor
Wood

Prior's
Grove

4   1 Northend
PH

Queen's
Wood

Cadyshute Way
Launder's
Farm

Holloway Lane

Watlington
Park

Fire
Wood   2

Hollandridge Lane

3

Greenfield

Hollandridge
Farm

B 481
To Nettlebed

College
Wood

Longhill
Hanging Wood

Ballam's Lane

B 480 To Stonor

1 Kilometre
1 mile

WALK 4

CHRISTMAS COMMON

3.5 miles (5 km)

This walk is mostly in woodland and passes through an area which was documented in a boundary charter dated 774 AD in which King Offa granted land, now Pyrton and part of Pishill and Stonor, to the Abbey of Worcester in the West Midlands.

1 SU728929

A mile (2 km) along the road from Christmas Common to Northend, at the end of the first group of houses, a public bridleway leads off to the right through a patch of woodland.

Most of the trees here are sycamore and in early summer the undersides of the leaves are often infested with sycamore aphids, one of the few insect species which feed on this tree. Individuals do not tolerate close body contact in the colony; look and see how they are spaced out very regularly to give each an area of 'personal space'. Winged adults are very sensitive to disturbance. If a leaf is touched the aphids quickly react and jump off. Each individual gives off an alarm smell so warning neighbours which results in a cloud of aphids flying off the leaf. Aphids are a rich food source for birds and this is a redeeming feature for the otherwise much maligned sycamore, disliked by conservationists because of its vigorous seeding (see later).

The trail emerges at Launder's Farm where a sign points left. The name of Launder's Farm preserves the name of this valley when, in 1270 it was recorded as Lavenoredene. The path continues down the valley, following the line of the county boundary, into woodland at the bottom.

2 SU727920

The woodland contains a varied flora including several species of grass and ferns. Wild relatives of raspberry and gooseberry can also be spotted alongside the path through the wood. The path is sunken in places and this indicates that it has been in use for a long time, probably linking Hollandridge Farm further along the trail with Northend.

In the valley bottom the path crosses a wider track. This is the Oxfordshire Way which follows the route of the 774 AD boundary charter mentioned earlier.

For an alternative route with a less steep climb, turn right here and follow the Oxfordshire Way up the valley to emerge from the woods turning right along the track just before point 4.

Most of the woodland is mature beech and ash, but sycamore is invading, notice the large numbers of saplings here. Sycamore was introduced to England in the fifteenth or sixteenth century and is now very common. It tends to compete with ash and beech and could in time become the dominant tree of Chiltern woodland.

In early summer, notice hoverflies hanging in the air in sunny patches in the wood. These are the male flies defending territories until females fly into the sunny areas. Speckled wood butterflies also occur here where the woodland is less dense. They are inhabitants of the woodland edge where their caterpillars feed on grass.

Continue up a short steep hill to emerge at the top into a large arable field covered with flints. Follow the path across the field to Hollandridge Farm.

Originally this large field was three smaller ones, two of which were called Upper and Lower Stockings according to a map of the Stonor Estate made in 1725. These names indicate that the fields were cleared directly from woodland.

3 SU726916

Hollandridge Farm dates back to at least 1282 when it was an outlying Pyrton manor owned by Emma Herlinggerrugge. A century later in 1387 it was recorded as belonging to William Harlyngrugge. The ponds which lie on the left of the path would have supplied the water for the livestock as there are no streams in this vicinity.

Turn right on to the road. This quiet road used to be the main Watlington–Henley route until about 1800, but has existed since prehistory as a ridgeway or 'Ruggeway' as it was known. It is the continuation of Knightsbridge Lane which travels the length of Pyrton parish (see Walks 3, 5 and 7). The lane is bordered by steep banks with many distinctive woodland plants as well as several different species of ferns and grasses, all easily visible. Also present are rosebay willow herb, bellflower and foxglove while in spring, bluebells can be seen in the hedge bottom. In places where the soil is very thin the flowering plants give way to mosses and lichens which can cope with much harsher conditions than can the plants.

4 SU717929

The alternative route rejoins the trail here. At the top of the lane look out for Priors Grove Cottage on the left and turn left down the gravel track running alongside the cottage. Almost at once take the path to the right into woodland.

Patches of soft rush, used in the past for floor covering and lamp wicks indicate that the ground here is damp. Nearby, the Saxon boundary charter recorded a pool, Lufa's mere, but there is no other sign of it now. In the summer the plants and grasses on the edge of the wood bear white frothy cuckoo spit which shelters the growing nymphs of froghoppers. These young insects feed from the water conducting tubes of the plants and blow bubbles into the excess water which they excrete so forming the froth. This woodland had been replanted with conifers so the ground flora is sparse. In early summer you may smell stinkhorn fungi, whose foetid odour attracts flies which spread their spores.

The path leads on to the road where the trail turns right past the Fox and Hounds pub which opens at traditional hours. The grassy area in front of the pub, which dates from the seventeenth century, was a pond until the early 1950s. Continue to the road junction and take the grassy track almost straight ahead.

5 SU715933

The hamlet of Christmas Common was, as its name suggests, part of an open area which until the early nineteenth century stretched for several miles. It linked common grazing land from Watlington Hill through Northend Common, where the walk started, to Turville Heath and Summer Heath, the last name implying a seasonal use for grazing. Prior to 1272 the area was larger but at this time the Earl of Cornwall was given permission to enclose part of this common waste as Watlington Park, a deer park. The Christmas part of the name is thought to be derived from the old Oxfordshire dialect name of Christmas tree for holly which is plentiful in the area.

The track passes Magpie Cottage and continues to the left past some small fields likely to be old enclosures taken from the common land. The trail turns right to enter woodland composed of mixed species including yew and oak, whose coppiced appearance indicates that this was once part of the common land. In early summer the new growth of the oaks may be severely damaged by the caterpillars of the winter moth. The moths emerge from the soil in the middle of winter when the wingless females crawl up the oak trees where they are found and mated by the flying males. The females then lay eggs on the buds of the oak which hatch in spring to coincide with the new growing leaves which they eat. By late spring or early summer, the fully grown larvae dangle on threads and drop to the ground to pupate until winter. The dense tangle of threads may be readily encountered as you walk through here at this time of the year.

In this part of the wood you may find foxgloves in midsummer. Look inside the flowers to see the dense patches of dark spots lining the flower tubes which serve to direct bees to the nectar at the base of the flower.

Keep to the main path and soon a distinct bank is reached. This shows the demarcation between the woodland managed for timber production and the old common land: look at the difference in the vegetation on each side. This difference in use is clearly shown on the 1797 map of Oxfordshire. The bank also marks the boundary between Pyrton and Shirburn parishes.

6 SU719935

Past the boundary bank, the path skirts some hollows in the ground which are probably old pits dug to extract chalk for liming fields or flint for road making. Compare them with a smaller old saw-pit which will soon be passed on the left when the path bears left downhill.

At first Shotridge Wood is typical beechwood but as the path descends it becomes more overgrown and the mixed vegetation suggests that this area was once more open, as grassland plants such as yellow rattle can be found. This plant is semi-parasitic on grass roots, and gets its name from the rattle of the ripe seeds in the dried pods.

The woody species are mixed as well with leathery leaved goat willow, dogwood and crab apple. On many of the small tree trunks and lower branches you will notice that the bark has been stripped off as a result of feeding by squirrels and deer. The thin sappy bark is a good food source for these animals at certain times of the year, whose feeding can cause severe damage and eventually death to branches or trunks if too extensive.

After half a mile (1 km) look out for small white arrows on a tree on the left indicating a narrow path turning right steeply uphill. Follow this path which soon widens and seems to follow an old route to the edge of the woodland.

At the edge of the wood a large crater-like hole can be seen, whose regular outline is unlike the hollows seen earlier. It may be a swallow hole, caused by the ground subsiding after an underground hole has developed in the chalk due to water action.

Cross the narrow field known as Wiggins Closes in 1759 and follow the track which leads to the road. Turn left along the road. As you return to your starting point look out for the old county boundary marker on the right hand side near the bus shelter.

Speckled Wood Butterfly

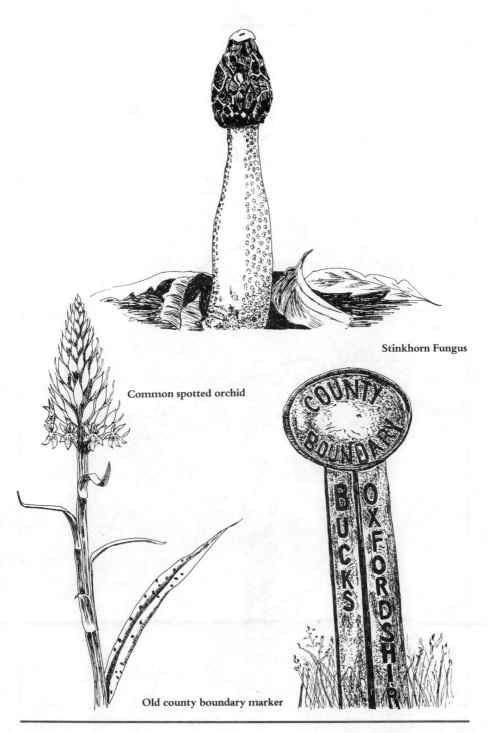

Stinkhorn Fungus

Common spotted orchid

Old county boundary marker

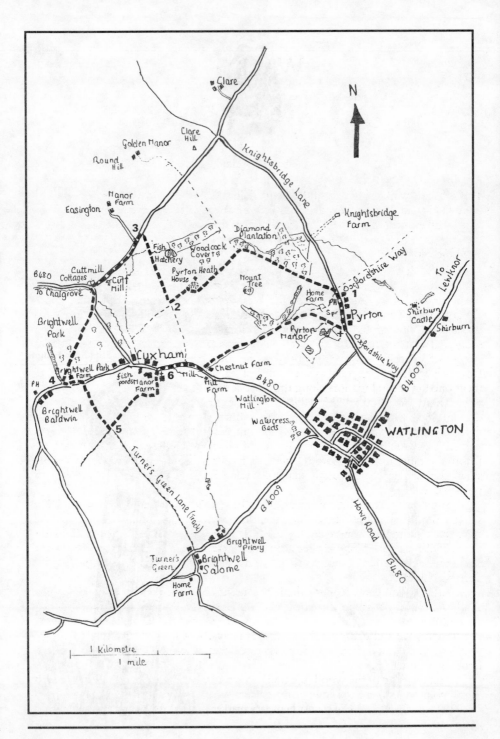

WALK 5

CUXHAM

6 miles (10 km)

This is a level walk using part of the Oxfordshire Way and following some of the old open-field boundaries of Cuxham, a village with extensive early records, many of which still exist in the care of Merton College, Oxford.

1 SU689961

Start the walk in Pyrton, taking the bridleway marked Oxfordshire Way just past Tara House next to The Plough public house. Pyrton is first documented as a Saxon estate granted by King Offa to the Bishop of Worcester. This quiet road, Knightsbridge Lane, was once a more important route, linking Henley to Worcester via an old route through Islip, north of Oxford (see Walks 3, 4 and 7). It has been suggested that the name of the road came from the guards on the bridge further along the road, possibly ancestors of the four freemen recorded here in the Domesday Book. Freemen were unusual in this part of England, but were mentioned in several manors along this part of the Chilterns.

The track follows a field edge where there are many species of grasses easily distinguished when flowering. Notice how tiny their seeds are in comparison with those of cultivated cereal grasses in adjacent fields. Horse tails grow in the field corner, members of a very ancient group of plants, fossils of which date back long before the dinosaurs. They are relations of ferns but see how the flowers resemble small cones. The coarse rough stems contain silica and were used in the past to polish silver.

Soon the track (which may be muddy here) follows the edge of a mixed wood on the right with large specimens of elderberry and field maple. Look for the attractive feathery silver-green leaves and yellow flowers of silverweed along the woodland edge. Many docks grow along the field edge, plants which favour disturbed agricultural ground, their seeds often inadvertently transported by farm machinery.

After a woodland strip on the left, a useful area of cover for gamebirds such as pheasant and partridge, the track reaches Diamond plantation, possibly named after Queen Victoria's Diamond Jubilee. At the corner of the field the trail turns left, leaving the Oxfordshire Way. At this point there is an enormous old cherry tree, covered with lichen which has a split trunk with the remains of a wild honey-bee nest.

Past the edge of the wood, the trail crosses a large field and skirts Pyrton Heath House following along the edge of the garden where you will pass a large old holly tree. Look at the lower leaves on the tree; many have light green and brown scarred patches in the centre caused by the maggot of a small fly, the holly leaf miner, burrowing inside. Some of the leaves may have a torn V-shaped cut made by blue tits feeding on the miners.

When you reach a concrete track turn left and continue until it bends to the left at the end of the hedge.

2 SU669960

At this junction turn sharp right and walk with the hedge on your right. The expanse of the fields must look very similar to the large open medieval fields which remained unchanged until they were enclosed in 1846/7. Many of the divisions made then have since been removed so once again there is an open vista in this area. In the Middle Ages, settlements had two or three large arable fields divided into furlongs, further split into strips which were held by different tenants. This immediate area was Cuxham's North Field or the 'field towards Pyrton' and the hedge line marks the boundary between Cuxham and Pyrton. Beyond the brow of the hill ahead lie Golder Manor and the small hamlet of Clare, all that remain of larger settlements which shrank due to the combined effects of the Black Death and early enclosure of the open fields in the fourteenth century, which reduced the land available for peasant cultivation.

Along the field edge look for feathery-leaved camomile and pineapple scented mayweed. Like dock, these are 'weeds of cultivation', growing in the regularly disturbed ground of ploughed fields, but rarely in the undisturbed hedgerows. You may also find field pansy with tiny yellow flowers and the blue germander speedwell or bird's eye. To the right a line of poplars shows where the ground conditions are more moist: poplars are not found on the well drained chalk of the Chiltern Hills.

By the poplars the path crosses through a gate and continues in the same direction as before but with the hedge on the left. This area is overgrown but the damp conditions make it an ideal site for meadowsweet with creamy plumes of flowers in late summer. This plant used to be collected for strewing on cottage floors, the sweet smell being released when they were walked on.

At a footbridge crossing a small stream, pause to notice the green plate-like growth of liverwort, which needs a damp habitat and the red roots of the overhanging pollard willow trees low on the banks. In the shade of the willows, stinging nettles grow, here tall, straggly thin-leaved plants compared with the dense patches of more substantial plants to be found in open sunny positions. Some of the leaves may be rolled up in the spring. They contain the caterpillars of the moth called Mother of Pearl, so named because of its pale colour.

The path emerges from the trees to a wetland area with reed beds, a good site for many birds and insects. If you are lucky you may hear the chirring song of reed buntings.

The path continues through a scrubby patch onto a field. Keeping the hedge on your left walk uphill for a short distance until a track leads down on the left to the road. Just before you descend to the road, look back at the old North Field where you have just walked. If conditions are suitable you may be able to pick out a ridge across the field, running parallel to the stream. This shows the boundary or baulk of two of the medieval furlongs, Butt Furlong and Town Mead Furlong. Closer

Silverweed

Reed Bunting

Cedar avenue in Brightwell Park

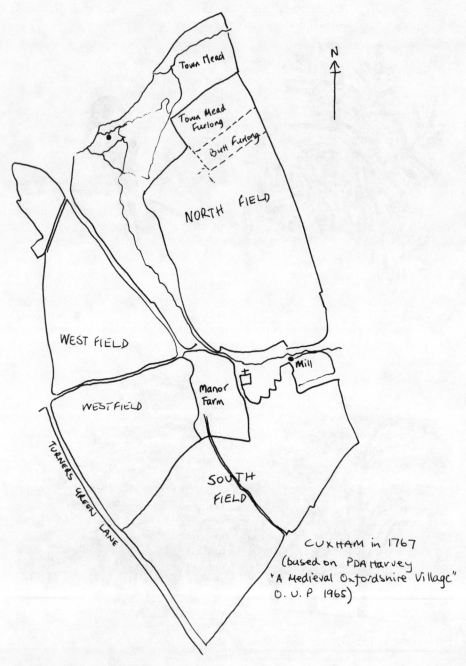

N

Town Mead

Town Mead Furlong

Butt Furlong

NORTH FIELD

WEST FIELD

Mill

WESTFIELD

Manor Farm

TURNERS GREEN LANE

SOUTH FIELD

CUXHAM in 1767
(based on PDA Harvey
"A Medieval Oxfordshire Village"
O.U.P 1965)

1767 Map of Cuxham's Fields

to the stream was Town Mead, meadow land for hay, which was divided in strips amongst the tenants, first allocated every year but later held permanently by each tenant.

3 SU666968

At the road turn left and walk with care along to the next junction where the trail turns left along the road signposted towards Cuxham and Watlington. To the left you will glimpse Cutt Mill, one of three mills mentioned in the Domesday Book at Cuxham, reflecting the plentiful water supply and fertile land of this area. A second is passed later in the walk, the third has disappeared. All were watermills, windmills were a later innovation.

After a short time a track goes off to the right where the road bends. Growing at this junction is horse-radish with large strong-smelling broad leaves, the roots of which are used in the traditional sauce.

Follow the track until it becomes more open. Across the fields to your left there is a view of Cuxham in the foreground with the Watlington white mark on the hill behind. Although this was designed to represent an obelisk, a local story says that it was made to give the illusion of a spire on the church in Watlington. At this point turn to the right through a gate. Cross the grass diagonally to the left towards a gate on a track and turn left. This old parkland belonged to Brightwell House, which was demolished in 1948 except for the kitchen wing and stables. The grassland in this field is sometimes dug for turf.

Continue to an avenue of impressive cedars, which originally led downhill to the house, and head slightly to the right towards the black and white cottage where the path leads through two small gates to the road.

4 SU656951

Turn left along the road. The village to the right is Brightwell Baldwin where there is a pub, The Lord Nelson (closed on Mondays). Along the road turn right up a track. This is another old route which has become less important, Turner's Green Lane leading to Britwell Salome. Its earlier width can be guessed from the fact that there is a holloway hidden in the undergrowth on the right where the path starts to climb, showing how much use this track once had.

On each side of the track there are many different flowering plants including the yellow agrimony and purple-flowered knapweed with both dog and field roses in the hedge. The chalky nature of the soil is apparent in the number of plant species growing here which like a high calcium concentration such as ladies bedstraw, black knapweed and field scabious. The soft earth makes for easy tunnelling by rabbits, their burrows are numerous on the right hand bank.

5 SU661947

When the track starts to narrow look out on the left for a stile, which is hidden in the hedge bank. Climb the stile and walk straight on keeping the hedge between two fields on your left. This hedge marks the sixteenth-century boundary between the West and South Fields, the other two arable fields of Cuxham, the West Field stretching beyond the track leading to Brightwell Park walked earlier and the South

Field continuing onto the ridge on your right. Along this hedge you may find some more 'weed' plants in the summer. Look out for field madder, with small purple flowers which was used as a dye to produce a rich red colour.

After a time the path passes the back of Manor Farm, the site of the medieval manor house. In the small field close by there are traces of the old track which led up to the South field shown by a flat-topped ridge in the grass. Beyond the present-day pond, a depression in the ground shows where the medieval fish pond lay.

Soon the path reaches a track and the trail turns left here to enter Cuxham village. In the Middle Ages, Cuxham belonged to Merton College in Oxford and many records still remain from those days in the form of manorial accounts and descriptions of the land held by the lord of the manor. It was a small parish and had to rely on neighbouring Pyrton for supplies of wood and hay, as well as having the use of some of Pyrton's common land on the Chiltern escarpment and possibly at Pyrton Heath. Cuxham had links with Ibstone in the Chiltern hills, which was also owned by the College and again wood was transported from there to Cuxham. Corn from Cuxham was sold in London and was transported via Henley down the Thames.

The church which is passed on the right is worth a visit with Norman architecture and a Jacobean pulpit.

6 SU667953

At the road, turn right through the village passing the Half Moon pub on the left. The picturesque roadside stream once powered the three Cuxham mills, one of which remains as the Old Mill House (the last house on the right) with a wooden platform and doors where corn and flour were hoisted and lowered.

Continue to Chestnut Farm and follow the sign for Pyrton, going left round some farm buildings to follow a stream on the right. On the banks look for pink flowered great willow herb and bur-reed, a flowering plant with iris-like leaves and green spiky fruits. See how plants like dog rose and elder sometimes grow in the crevices of the pollarded willows bordering the stream, the seeds carried there by birds sheltering in the thick new growth of twigs. A conspicuous red and black jumping froghopper may be seen on the vegetation in early summer. It is a relative of the insects which produce cuckoo spit, but its young stages live underground, sucking juices from plant roots, and so do not need to produce the frothy spit for protection.

Continue until you come to a farm bridge over a wide ditch and then turn right over a metal stile, walking up the field parallel to the hedge before turning diagonally to aim for the small brick house at the right-hand corner of the field.

The large trees on the right hide Pyrton Manor, built by Edmund Symeon, the father-in-law of John Hampden, a Parliamentarian Civil War leader. Earlier in its history, the manor was held by the Black Prince and by Henry V.

At the corner of the field climb the stile, turn left along the track past the church. Go left at the road, back to the start.

Cuxham Church

Fruiting Bur-reed

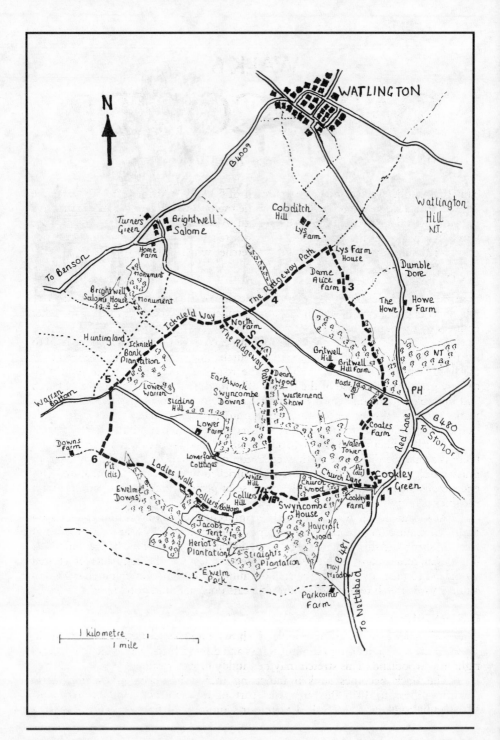

WALK 6
SWYNCOMBE

6.5 miles (10 km)

This trail can be walked in two parts, each of 5 miles (8 km), if shorter walks are desired or as a single longer walk. Part of the trail follows one of the most attractive parts of the Ridgeway long distance footpath. Although it descends and ascends the Chiltern escarpment the paths chosen are not too steep and the going underfoot is good for the most part, with only a few stretches which may be muddy.

1 SU695902

Start the walk at Cookley Green. Along one side of the Green notice the distinctive line of scots pines, one of our three native conifers, easily distinguished from other conifers by the orange bark on new growth at the top of the trees.

Look for the War Memorial at the south end of the Green and take the road to the right of the one marked Swyncombe Church. The cricket pitch will be seen over the hedge on the left. On each side of the road are fine specimens of lime with twiggy growth at the base of the trunks. The road passes through an area of beech and bramble woodland which in spring has a colourful display of flowers. These plants generally flower before the trees are in leaf to overshadow them, the seeds quickly maturing and ripening before the tree shading becomes thicker.

A little further on, the right-hand side of the road borders agricultural land and there is a marked difference in the vegetation on this side of the road with coarser grasses and weeds where the soil has been enriched with fertilizers or manure. This encourages the ranker growth at the expense of plants which cannot compete with the thicker growth.

At Coates Farm, which, in the late eighteenth century, was known as Bacon Farm, continue along the road. The hedges on each side are rich in many species of tree and shrub and this variety can be useful in dating the age of the hedge. However in the Chilterns many hedges were formed by leaving the remnants of cleared woodland to form a barrier so the rule of thumb approximation that each species in a thirty yard stretch represents a hundred years does not hold good here.

2 SU697912

The road passes a small area of woodland, shown on Davis's map of Oxfordshire in 1797. At the road junction go straight across and down a bridleway which then bears right into woodland. This stretch may be muddy in wet weather.

The track becomes sunken indicating that it has been in use for many centuries. Prior to 1815 this area was part of the common land belonging to Watlington parish and was called Seymour Common or Seamer Green. It was a mixture of pasture and woodland used for grazing sheep and in the past was linked with the large area of common at Maidens Grove, now Russell's Water Common, where Watlington also had grazing rights (Walks 7 and 9). The presence of many old coppiced trees shows that wood was cut here in the past, the trees being allowed to regrow to provide more smallwood for fuel, fencing and repairs.

In autumn, this path is thick with the fallen beech leaves which often cover and shade out small herbs leaving the characteristic bare ground of beech woods. Look out for candle snuff fungus with white powdery tips on the dead cut beech stumps.

Through the trees to the right as you descend the hill you have a good view of Howe Farm, which, it is thought, is the site of an ancient manor of Watlington called Hoo named from the Old English 'hoh' meaning a ridge.

3 SU692926

The path becomes a wider level track and soon reaches Dame Alice Farm which, in the fourteenth century, was connected with Alice, Duchess of Suffolk, who was a grand-daughter of Geoffrey Chaucer, the author of *The Canterbury Tales*. She endowed the impressive brick-built school and almshouses which still remain in nearby Ewelme. This farm, part of which dates from the sixteenth century, is on the site of another hamlet called Anthills, recorded during the thirteenth and fourteenth centuries but later abandoned as a result of early enclosure of the land for sheep pasture.

Along this section of the trail there are fine views to the right of the National Trust downland at Watlington Hill, a notable beauty spot and viewpoint.

Continue along the track until it reaches the road, then turn left past a brick and flint gateway along the Ridgeway (Icknield Way: see Introduction). The trail passes through a leafy corridor for about half a mile (1 km) where the path is overhung with tall shrubs of hazel and privet. Buckthorn provides leafy food for the caterpillars of the yellow brimstone butterfly which is often one of the first to be seen in spring, although it flies all summer. Coppiced whitebeam is also found, its leaves a characteristic silver-white colour on the underside. On the ground, look for violets which border the track. Soon the path becomes a wide grassy track, an ideal spot to pause and watch bees and butterflies visiting the numerous wild flowers along this most attractive stretch of the Ridgeway.

4 SU681922

The trail crosses a road which climbs in a straight line up the hill. All the land to the left of the Ridgeway, now arable fields, is shown as rough downland on the map of 1797 but aerial photographs show traces of Iron Age fields to the left of the road on the slope, showing how land usage changes over the centuries in response to local needs and abilities. The road itself is interesting. The part on the left-hand slope was an old track but that to the right was only formed as a result of the Parliamentary Enclosures in 1845. The presence of wide grass verges and the straightness of this road shows how the track was improved and extended to link the top of the hills directly with Brightwell Salome.

Continue along the Ridgeway until North Farm is reached.

Candle Snuff Fungus

Sainfoin

St Botolph's Church, Swyncombe

SHORT CUT At North Farm the Ridgeway turns left and for a shorter walk this route can be taken to join with the remainder of the trail at Swyncombe Church at point 7 (for description see text at end of walk).

Continue along the Icknield Way, which here is also part of Swanns Way, a modern long-distance bridleway linking the Salcey Forest in north Buckinghamshire with Goring-on-Thames.

On the hill to the right is Britwell House built in 1728. The stone column was erected in 1764 by Sir Edward Simeon in memory of his parents. On a clear day the twentieth-century cooling towers of Didcot Power Station ten miles away and the tree-topped Iron Age fort of Wittenham Clumps can be seen ahead. Rising to the left is Swyncombe Down which is not open to the public. It is topped with a system of banks and ditches thought to be either Bronze Age or Anglo-Saxon in origin, the extent of which is clearly shown on the Ordnance Survey map. Some of these may be seen along the short cut.

Soon a strip of beech woodland on the left is reached called Icknield Bank Plantation, planted since the end of the eighteenth century on land which was previously rough downland grazing. Look for brown patches on the beech leaves in summer. These are caused by larvae of the beech-leaf miner beetle which tunnel through and eat the leaf tissue.

5 SU666914

At the road, walk with care straight on for about a hundred yards, then turn left following a bridleway beside a thick hedge along a field edge. This hedgerow contains several shrub species including spindle. This is used as a food plant by the caterpillars of the small ermine moth which live together in a thick protective silk webbing covering large sections of hedge showing where the caterpillars have eaten the leaves and moved on to new patches.

Swyncombe Down can be seen across the valley to your left. Part of the slope is called Lower Warren and was probably used as a rabbit warren in the past. Rabbits were introduced by the Normans for food and were kept in artificial warrens for hundreds of years only becoming a pest in the wild in the nineteenth century.

At the top of a small rise, the path veers towards another hedge and the first, which marks a parish boundary, follows a characteristically sinuous line downhill to the left. There may be areas of rough ground at the corner of the fields here and elsewhere along the trail. These provide cover for game birds such as partridge and pheasant, also introduced species, and often are planted with sunflowers or cabbages which, while providing food for adult birds, act as a habitat for insects vital for successful chick rearing.

6 SU663906

When the path reaches a farm road turn left uphill, past a variety of planted trees including laburnum whose small black seeds are poisonous. The small, glossy evergreen shrub is spurge laurel which may have been planted here but which occurs naturally in areas of old woodland. Sycamore is invading the woodland here and its leaves are often covered by black patches of tar-spot fungus.

Look out for a yellow bridleway sign to the left into woodland just before the road bends and follow this for a short distance. The track emerges from the woodland and follows the edge of a field up the valley which is a good example of the typical land formation of Chiltern valleys with the south-facing slopes (ie the one opposite) being markedly steeper than the north-facing slope. It is thought that this difference resulted from alternate freezing and thawing action during the Ice Age.

In the summer the woods ahead may show the cumulative effect of acid rain and age by their yellow or chlorotic leaves, a symptom which is made worse by periods of drought as in 1976 and 1989. The line of tall lime trees in the foreground marks the route which in the past was an approach to Swyncombe House ahead.

The track becomes wooded on the right and here is called Collier's Bottom, a reference to charcoal burners. As you walk, notice the line of stately horse chestnut trees planted in the nineteenth century, ideal now for conker collecting in the autumn.

7 SU682902

The track leads past Swyncombe House. (The shorter route rejoins the main trail here.) The present house was rebuilt fairly recently but prior to this there was a succession of houses on the site. A Tudor manor house was burnt down in 1814 and later replaced during the mid-nineteenth century before again being damaged by fire a hundred years later. The manor was recorded in the Domesday Book as being held by Miles Crispin who gave it to the monks of the Abbey of Bec in Normandy who held it until 1410. There seems to have been a settlement here in those times as in 1279 twenty-one households were recorded. However nothing now remains of the hamlet except St Botolph's church which is early Norman in origin and well worth a visit. From the outside, zig-zag patterns in the flints which make up the walls can be seen, a typical Norman design, as is the rounded end or apse.

After leaving the church take the footpath behind it through the churchyard and turn left onto a grassy track. Enter a field and cross towards the wood making for a white gate. Looking back, the landscaped park around Swyncombe House can be seen. The wood is now known as Church Wood but the first edition Ordnance Survey map published in 1830 calls this New Copse. However the ground flora would indicate that this is an old wood so this previous name is puzzling. Some fairly recent conifer planting has been carried out in some parts of the wood. The path emerges on the road where the trail turns right to return to Cookley Green and your starting point.

SHORT CUT 4.5 miles (7 km)
6 SU678921 *At North Farm turn left and follow the track past the brick farm buildings. The edge on the left contains several flowering plants including a pink vetch-like flower called sainfoin which was grown as crop for animal feed. It was also used to improve the soil quality as, like other members of the pea family, it is able to convert nitrogen from the air into a form which can be stored in nodules on the plant's roots. When a sainfoin crop is ploughed in, the nitrogen is then available for the next crop.*

The path climbs uphill and bears to the right to enter woodland called Dean Wood. The bank which can be seen on the left marks the boundary between Watlington and Swyncombe parishes, but a little further on the path crosses a parallel bank and ditch earthwork, part of the system on Swyncombe Down.

After this the trail passes through more modern woodland probably planted in the nineteenth century, possibly as a result of the agricultural depression. See if you can discover differences in the appearance of this newer woodland and the old woodland you have seen elsewhere. The path then follows a field edge down and uphill to reach a road leading to Swyncombe Church where the main trail is met at point 7.

Yellow archangel

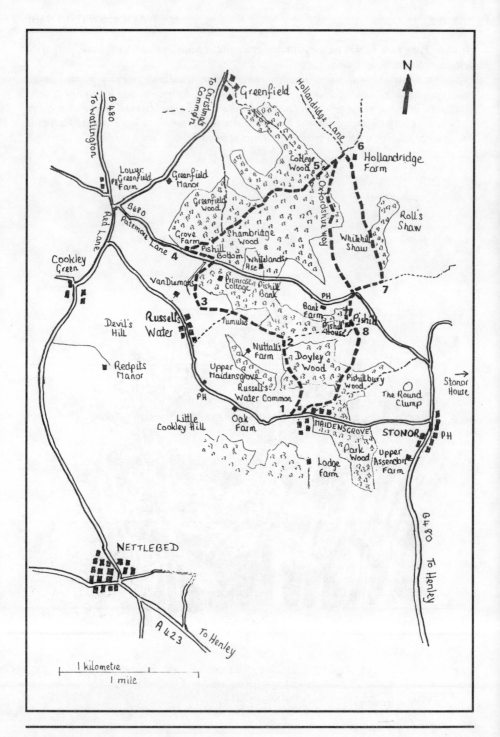

WALK 7

PISHILL

5 miles (8 km)

This trail passes through secluded landscapes which change from open and wooded common land to farmland and beech woodland, some managed by the Forestry Commission. There are wide-ranging views along the walk but there are also some steep climbs through the woods. This, and the next two trails explore the landscape around Russell's Water Common.

1 SU720888

Start on Russell's Water Common at Maidensgrove and take the track to the left across the common to Maidensgrove Farm. Go over the stile opposite you across the farmyard and follow the fenced path through a horse paddock. Climb another stile into woodland and continue along this path as it descends to the valley bottom and climbs through the wood to a field.

This wood is called Doyley Wood, named after the D'Oilly family who held the manor of Pishill Napper in the Middle Ages. They were an important famiy with land and connections all over Oxfordshire. There is a rich woodland flora here which indicates the great age of the wood. Look out for wood spurge, sanicle, woodruff and wood rush which grows in clumps on the barer ground. On the right some replanting has taken place with larch and cyprus. In the open areas silver birch is colonizing and there are plants such as foxglove and coltsfoot which prefer a more open habitat. On dewy autumn days the silvery spider's webs are particularly attractive on the holly bushes.

2 SU719896

Emerging from the wood, bear left around the field edge. In the spring notice how bluebells are growing in the hedge bottom on the left, a sign that this field was cleared directly from woodland in the past. To the right is a distant view of the park which surrounds Stonor House.

When you reach the wood turn left. This path links Pishill and Russell's Water, which in the past was called Pishill Venables and was probably a church path as it leads directly to the church at Pishill. You will pass a pond to the left where wild mallard duck may be nesting.

Soon the path is more open. Along this stretch notice the hedgerow plants and as you approach some farm buildings see how the vegetation changes to agricultural weeds such as chickweed, docks, hemp nettle and stinging nettle, all plants which like a rich soil and can tolerate disturbed conditions.

Past the farm buildings on the left in a group of beech trees is a large Bronze

Age tumulus or burial mound topped by two huge cherry trees.

Follow the track over the common to the edge of the bracken and scrubby woodland. There are wide views here to the left over the common which until the end of the eighteenth century was part of a huge area of common land extending from the far side of Maidensgrove (Walk 9) to the escarpment above Watlington (Walk 6). On Davis's map made in 1797 this part of the common was called Minney or Maiden Grove.

The heather, gorse and bracken growing in this area show that the soil here is acidic due to the clay laid down on top of the chalk. The pits which can be seen if you explore off the path are the remains of those dug to extract the clay and sand for the brick-works which were at Russell's Water by at least 1665 and continued in use until the end of the nineteenth century.

At the edge of the scrubby woodland turn right and follow the edge of the open grassland. To your left the ground is carpeted with bluebells and white wood anemones in May.

3 SU709900

After 500 yards (400 m) when the path reaches the far corner of the common turn left into the woodland and follow the path downhill to the road. As you walk notice that there is a mixture of species here including oak, beech and hazel, many of which have been coppiced in the past when this was part of the common. Compare this varied appearance with that of the typical beechwoods which will be reached in a while.

When the road is reached turn left. Walk with care as the traffic is fast here.

4 SU708905

After about 500 yards (400 m) look for a tall pair of iron gates on the right marked Grove Farm opposite Woodman's Cottage. Go through the gates and follow the arrows across the yard and uphill into Shambridge Wood. Although in the past this old wood would have contained a mixture of species like the area of old common seen earlier, it is obvious that now there is only beech with a little holly. Over the last two hundred years beech was encouraged and planted to provide timber for the furniture industry and it is this interference by man which has resulted in single species woodland. The dense shade and thin flinty soil discourages any ground flora.

Keep straight on when a path branches off to the left. As the path descends look out for an oval saw-pit on the right, its banks covered with mosses. Large two-man saws were used in the saw pits to cut the beech trunks into planks in the woods for ease of transport. The saw-men who worked here were called the top-dog, the boss, and the one in the pit having to put up with sawdust falling on him and difficult working conditions was the under-dog, usually an apprentice.

A little further on there is a larch plantation which acts as a nurse crop protecting young deciduous species such as ash, cherry, rowan and beech.

At the top of the hill bear right then left downhill. In this area in late spring you will notice the scaly fronds of the so-called male fern which uncoil as they emerge from the ground in contrast to the bracken whose young shoots resemble shepherds' crooks with a coiled end on a stalk.

Woodland track near Russell's Water Common

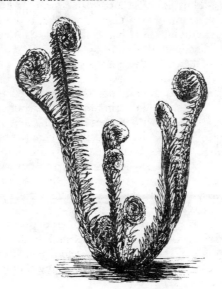

Male fern uncoiling

Hollandridge Lane

Go straight on at the next junction, following the path marked as W21 uphill. As the track climbs through this open area the flora changes again with plants which like open conditions such as wild strawberry, foxgloves and St John's Wort, an upright plant with yellow flowers. If you pick a leaf and hold it up to the light you will see tiny holes which, according to an old belief, ooze blood on 29 August, the day St John the Baptist was executed.

The path bears to the right following the white arrows, into a plantation of young beech. This may be a good place to see speckled wood butterflies where the woodland is not too thick. The males engage in territorial contests for ownership of the sunny spots, these being good mating places. Look out for wild raspberry canes and blue flowered bugle. After a time the woodland changes to more mature cover, the change marked by a large yew tree and the recurrence of more woodland plants, including primroses.

Continue following the white arrows and the obvious path.

5 SU723914

When an open glade is reached, cross diagonally to the left and take the narrow path on the right which climbs uphill. This part of the wood is full of flowers in the spring with a thick carpet of bluebells and woodsorrel flourishing where there are gaps in the thick overhead canopy.

SHORT CUT As the trail reaches a stile at the top of the wood, a path (the Oxfordshire Way), goes off to the right. This can be followed if an alternative route is required and meets the trail at point 7.

The field ahead was called Gully Piddle according to a map dated 1725. Piddle is a corruption of 'pightle' meaning a small piece of land and Gully describes the lie of the land. On the skyline to the right the two impressive trees in flower in May are wild cherry, a frequent sight in the Chilterns in spring.

Climb the stile and walk across the field to another stile in the far right hand corner. Over this, turn right along the track.

6 SU726916

The farm on the left is Hollandridge Farm which is also seen on the Christmas Common Walk (4). The impressive barns, granary and stable date from the early eighteenth century and appear on the Stonor estate map of 1725. The huge oak at the side of the track just before the gateway probably predates these buildings.

Continue along this track for some distance. Soon you will pass a large patch of garlic mustard which is a food plant of the caterpillar of the easily recognizable orange-tip butterfly.

The track passes between steep banks and in some places the soil has eroded away, exposing the tree roots. The shallow soil can be seen, lying on top of the upper chalk with bands of flints. The great amount of erosion here where the road leaves the clay-with-flints cap and cuts down the chalk slope towards the river at Henley-on-Thames shows the immense age of this route which ran the length of the old Pyrton parish and linked the river with the route to Worcester, an important centre in the days when its Archbishop held land as far away as the Chilterns (Walks 3 and 4).

After the woodland is left behind look out for a path to the right, but before you turn pause to look at the view to the left. The sinuous line of a track in the valley marks the county boundary between Buckinghamshire and Oxfordshire and also the line of the ancient boundary of Pyrton parish and Hundred which used to cover all this area. On the slope opposite, the regular fields show that they were laid out during the process of Parliamentary Enclosure around the beginning of the nineteenth century while to the right can be seen the eighteenth-century landscaped parkland of Stonor House with its specimen trees which replaced the earlier medieval hunting park situated close to Doyley Wood.

7 SU730902

Take the path to the right and follow it over stiles, past farm buildings. Look up to the right for a view of the track on the ridge. Turn left onto a track, the Oxfordshire Way (where the alternative route rejoins the main trail). At the road, turn right for a short distance before turning left up the road to the church.

Pishill (pronounced Pish-ill) even today only consists of a small hamlet. Its name means 'hill on which peas grow' which suggests that in Anglo-Saxon times the soil was deemed unsuitable for most crops. The church was originally built in the mid-twelfth century but was rebuilt by Rev Ruck Keene of Swyncombe House in 1854 (Walk 6). Behind the vicarage further along the road are the remains of a medieval building which is possibly part of the D'Oilly's manor house of Pishill Napper.

8 SU727897

Follow the yellow arrow signs for the Oxfordshire Way to the left; the path going off to the right is the church path from Russell's Water. Following the field edge go straight on downhill and then entering the woods, continue up a steep hill following the arrows. The banks which may be seen mark the boundary between Doyley and Pishillbury Woods. As the top is reached notice how oak trees grow here with the beech. Oak cannot tolerate chalky soil so they only occur in any numbers on the clay-with-flints capping on the hill tops. The path becomes muddy in this section, another sign of the water-impervious clay!

Keep straight on with the woodland edge on the right. A smell of garlic shows the presence of ramsons which flowers in the spring with white flowers clustered on the top of the stalk, another indicator of old woodland.

At a junction of the paths take the one to the right over a bank through shrubs to emerge on a small gravel road past cottages and houses. The pond which is passed could be the same as one used as a marker for the boundary of the old manor of Minigrove.

Return to the common turning right to return to the starting point.

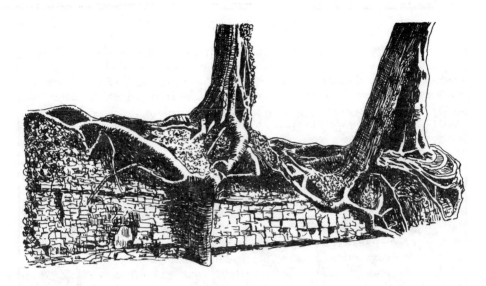

Chalk and flint profile

Pishill Church

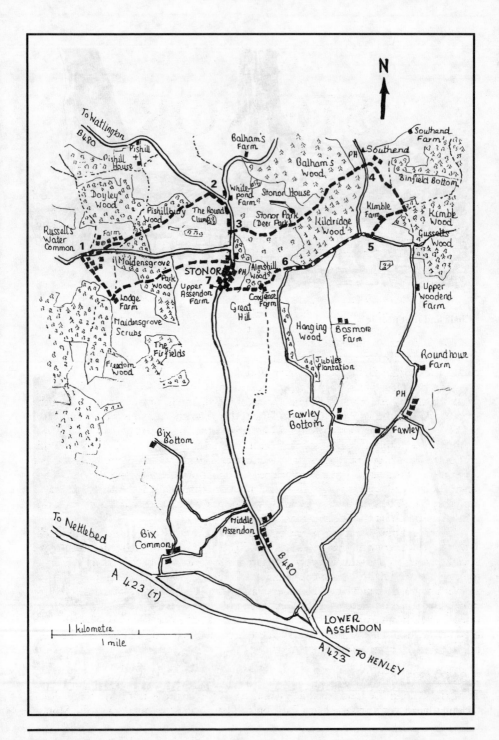

N

To Watlington
B480
Pishill
Pishill House
Doyley Wood
Russell's Water Common
Pishillbury Wood
The Round Clump
Balham's Farm
White-pond Farm
Stonor House
Stonor Park (Deer Park)
Balham's Wood
PH Southend
Southend Farm
Binfield Bottom
Kimble Farm
Kildridge Wood
Kimble Wood
Gussetts Wood
Maidensgrove
Park Wood
Lodge Farm
Maidensgrove Scrubs
The Firfields
Freedom Wood
STONOR
PH
Almshill Wood
Upper Assendon Farm
Coxlease Farm
Great Hill
Upper Woodend Farm
Hanging Wood
Basmore Farm
Jubilee Plantation
Roundhouse Farm
PH
Fawley Bottom
Fawley
Bix Bottom
To Nettlebed
Bix Common
Middle Assendon
B480
A 423 (T)
LOWER ASSENDON
A 423 TO HENLEY

1 kilometre
1 mile

1 2 3 4 5 6 7

WALK 8

STONOR

5.5 miles (9 km)

This walk links with the Pishill and Bix walks, the three covering a large area around Russell's Water Common. There are fine views, first of the parkland around Stonor, then of the house itself and further along the trail a wide landscape over the Thames valley. The scenery of rolling hills on these plateau walks contrasts with the steep scarp slope seen at Crowell, Shirburn and Swyncombe.

1 SU720888

Start on Russell's Water Common near Maidensgrove Farm. Go past the first footpath sign, head down the road towards Maidensgrove and then take the track to the left. A boggy pond is soon passed on the left. Keep along the track past houses and take the narrow path at the end marked with a white arrow. Once in the wood turn left and follow the arrows straight on at the next junction (path PS 9). The path curves to the right through Pishillbury Wood.

On the right-hand side there is a boundary bank and further on another joins from the left. These marked different areas of management or ownership within the woodland, but the one on the right is possibly also the remains of the medieval Stonor park boundary which was situated adjacent to this wood.

Although most of the trees are beech there are a number of cherry trees in this part of the wood. In spring they are easily distinguished by their white blossom, but the smooth, horizontally marked bark readily identifies them during the rest of the year. As the path starts to go downhill it passes through a less managed area of woodland with oak, ash, cherry and hazel, species which all occur naturally in this area when beech has not been actively encouraged.

As conditions become more open look at the grasses bordering the track. When in flower try and find the heads of tall couch grass with the seeds sticking out at right angles to the stem making a square fat head. Run your fingers up the stalks to compare this with the smaller rye-grass where seed clusters grow in line with the stem making a flattened head. Another plant to notice is hogweed, so named for the unpleasant smell of the crushed leaves. However, the flowers are very attractive to insects; in early summer see how many small black pollen beetles feed at the flowers together with numerous flies, wasps and other insects although butterflies, bumble bees and honey bees do not like them.

2 SU734893

Turn right along the road, walking with care as the traffic is fast here. Keep along the main road with Stonor Deer Park on the left. Soon the main gates for Stonor

House are passed. The House is well worth a visit and is open at certain times in the summer (for details telephone 049–163 587). Continue along the road a little further until you reach a path to the left through the railings into the deer park. Follow this, keeping dogs on leads.

3 SU737886

The path climbs uphill to start with, then follows the line of the hill up the valley. There are good views of Stonor House. The first written record of Stonor occurs as Stanora Lege (stony slope) in the charter of King Offa in 774 when it was part of a much larger Pyrton parish (see Walk 4). The Stonor family got their name from the place and can trace their ancestry from Robert de Stanora c.1150–1185. Since then the family have lived here for eight hundred years in unbroken succession. During the Reformation in the sixteenth century, the Stonors, in common with some other old families in this area, remained faithful to the Catholic Church despite severe penalties which lasted for a hundred and fifty years. They provided a hiding place for many priests, notably Edmund Campion who had a secret printing press here.

The house itself is based on a medieval core which has been altered and extended over the centuries. In 1416 the chapel tower was built with 200 000 bricks from Crocker End and by the end of the sixteenth century the house had been made into an E-shaped Tudor building. The next big change took place in the eighteenth century when the house was given its present form, again with locally made bricks supplied by Catherine Shurfield whose descendants still live in this area. The existing parkland dates from the same period, replacing the less ornamental deer park of the Middle Ages beside Pishillbury Wood walked through earlier.

Notice how the grass in the parkland is short, grazed by the fallow deer. Occasional tall individual plants with large, broad spear-shaped leaves at the edge of the path are poisonous deadly nightshade, whose bitter leaves protect it from grazing.

Like rabbits, fallow deer were probably introduced by the Normans in the early twelfth century as a food source which could utilize poor land. They were kept in deer parks, first for the hunt and later, as here, for decorative purposes. Fallow deer are now naturalized in the countryside at large, having escaped from parks. They can cause a lot of damage to woodland as they nibble young shoots; notice how the saplings in the park are protected by fences. In the rutting season in October and throughout the winter the does and bucks herd together, but keep apart in the summer when the fawns are born. You may notice occasional white animals, which are quite common in parkland herds. In the wild white animals are rare as they are so conspicuous to predators and hunters.

Along the path you will pass large clumps of brambles which in summer are full of bumble bees feeding at the flowers. The rich nectar source also attracts butterflies like the meadow brown, the darker coloured ringlet, the large and the small skipper, whose wings stick out at right angles to each other, the black and white marbled white tends to prefer grassland flowers so does not feed here.

The path continues and after a time goes through the deer fence and into Kildridge Wood. There are large clumps of rhododendron here originally planted for cover for game birds but now naturalized in many places where it has become a

Stonor House

Fallow Deer

Broad-leaved
Helleborine Orchid

Upper Assendon farm buildings

serious threat to native woodland. Its dense growth shades out woodland plants and its tenacity makes it difficult to eradicate, needing to be cut, poisoned or burnt for complete removal.

After a time the path bears left and joins an old track which leads from Stonor House to the hamlet of Southend. Kildridge Wood is an ancient wood with records dating back to 1439 when acorns for pigs and underwood (coppiced wood for fuel and repairs) were sold. In 1525 it was described as having 'beech, ash, witch elms, maple, aspen and whitebeam' but now it is mostly replanted with conifers. For a time the rights in the wood were held by Adrian Scrope of Wormsley, the grandfather of one of the men who signed the death warrant of Charles I.

As the track reaches a field edge on the left, so the trail crosses into Buckinghamshire.

4 SU752896

The trail crosses straight over a road, once a drovers road used by cattle and sheep drovers on their journeys from Wales to London or from the Wiltshire Downs to Thetford market in Norfolk. A former public house in Southend to the left was called The Drovers, a good indication of the trade of the majority of its customers.

Follow the trail over the stile and across the field. There are wide views of the Chiltern plateau to the left. Climb over another stile into woodland and go downhill to a track in the valley bottom. Here turn right and walk past Kimble Farm.

A large pond is situated on the parish boundary between Turville and Hambledon and could date from the distant past when scarce resources had to be shared. The oak tree on the left of the track probably acted as a boundary marker.

5 SU753889

At the road, turn right and continue straight on at the junction. This road is not as old as the other routes you follow along this trail. It was made some time after about 1830, probably at the time of local Parliamentary Enclosure. The woodland on the right is now part of Kilridge Wood, but this area has been planted with sweet chestnut possibly at the time the road was made. This tree is not a native species but is long established in England probably having been introduced by the Romans. It is not a good timber tree as it tends to develop deep cracks so it is difficult to obtain large planks, but its durability makes it suitable for fencing. The woods are attractive in spring when the trees bear long tassles of male flowers.

On the left are extensive views to the hills on the far side of Henley-on-Thames and beyond. At the bend in the road near the woodland edge look out for a bank in the woodland which marks the county boundary so that you are now once again in Oxfordshire. The clump of trees on the left shows the site of a Bronze Age burial mound.

6 SU744885

At a sharp left bend in the road carry straight on down a farm track leading to Coxlease Farm marked as a bridleway to Stonor. On the right the high fence bounds the edge of Stonor deer park. Follow the track to the left and walk between the farm buildings. Turn right at the end of a barn, keeping a tall conifer hedge on your left.

In a field behind the barn, notice an unusual brick-built granary, perched on columns to keep the grain out of the damp and to protect it against vermin.

The trail continues along this path into woodland and then turns sharply downhill along a path to the right. This is Almshill Wood and may have had links with the alms houses in Stonor village, the first of which were built before 1421. You may spot the uncommon broad-leaved helleborine orchid as well as the increasingly less common primrose. Notice that some of the trees here are yew, a native conifer.

The path continues over a stile and across a field to reach the road where you turn right.

7 SU735883

The trail passes Upper Assendon Farm with buildings dating from the seventeenth century. Look at the construction of the cow-shed and notice how the vertical supports are placed on stone pillars topped by cross grained timber to keep the uprights dry.

The village now known as Stonor was called Upper Assendon until 1896, this name dating from before the Norman conquest and meaning 'Assa's valley'. Middle and Lower Assendon still remain lower down the valley towards Henley-on-Thames.

Not far past the Stonor Arms, which requests walkers to remove muddy boots, look for Well Cottage on the left-hand side of the road and take the path at the side of the garden. Walk uphill, crossing two stiles. This field was called Little Park in the nineteenth century and the large one to the right edged by woodland, Great Park, shows the whereabouts of the medieval Stonor park.

Pause to look back for a dramatic view of Stonor House, the park and the village below. Head for Park Wood at the top of the hill, the stile marked by a large ash. Inside the wood, creeping yellow pimpernel can be found alongside the path, while the damp cool conditions are favourable for the growth of bright green clumps of sedges, easily distinguished from grasses by their triangular ridged stems. In summer look out for dark brown male speckled wood butterflies which may compete for ownership of the warm patches where females can be courted.

8 SU724884

Follow the path, over a stile and across a field. At the corner climb another stile on the left and take the short track between Lodge Farm and a cottage. At the tarmac lane, turn right and follow it back to Maidensgrove and your starting point.

Lodge Farm

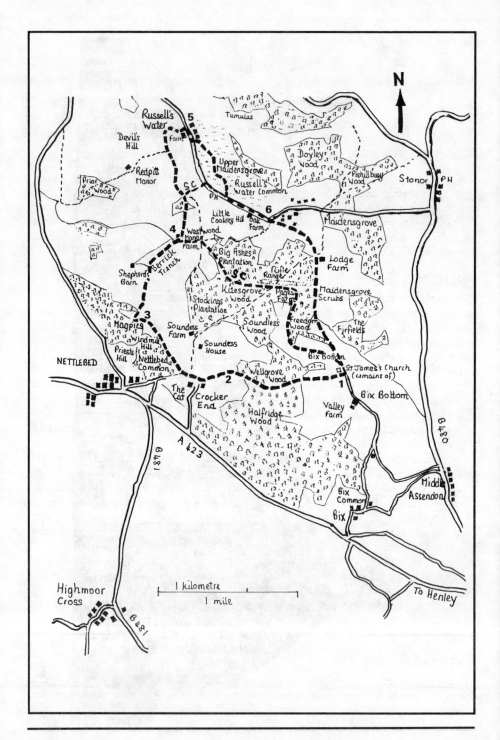

N

Tumulus

Russell's Water

5

Farm

Devil's Hill

Upper Maidensgrove

Doyley Wood

Pishill bury Wood

Stonor PH

Redpits Manor

Prior's Wood

SC

PH

Russell's Water Common

Maidensgrove

6

Little Cookley Hill

Oak Farm

4

Westwood Manor Farm

Big Ashes Plantation

Lodge Farm

Derrick Trench

SC

Rifle Range

Maidensgrove Scrubs

Shepherd's Barn

Kitesgrove Wood

Pages Farm

Stockings Wood Plantation

Soundess Farm

Soundless Wood

Freedom Wood

The Firfields

3

Magpies

Windmill Hill

Priests Hill

Nettlebed Common

Soundess House

Bix Bottom

NETTLEBED

2

Wellgrove Wood

St. James's Church (remains of)

1

Bix Bottom

The Cat

Crocker End

Halfridge Wood

Valley Farm

A 423

A 4130

Bix Common

Middle Assendon

Bix

To Henley

Highmoor Cross

B 481

1 kilometre

1 mile

80

WALK 9
BIX

6.5 miles (10.5 km) short cut 5 miles (8 km)

Starting from the ruins of a Norman church, this trail leads through an area of a once important local brick and pottery industry before following the line of an old track through a quiet valley up to a stretch of open common land. The trail returns to the start along the edge of a nature reserve. This walk links with Walks 7 and 8 at Russell's Water Common. There is a short cut which leads through the reserve.

1 SU727870

The starting point of this trail is the ruined Norman church of St James at Bix Bottom. In the Domesday Book this area was held by Hervey the papal legate who also held land ten miles away to the north at Ibstone, Buckinghamshire. Interestingly the churches in both places were almost identical, the one at Ibstone still being in use. Later this part of Bix was called Bix Brand after the holder of the manor in 1223, who also held land at Cuxham (Walk 5). It is not certain if there was ever a settlement here as the inhabitants possibly lived in isolated farms amongst the woods. The church was always very poor and was finally abandoned in 1875.

Take the track which climbs uphill along a field edge behind the church. Look out for an unusual coppiced ash in the hedge on the left which has formed a circle of regrowth after repeated cutting over the centuries.

Follow the path straight on as it leads through Wellgrove Wood, which is a mixture of beech, hazel coppice, oak and cherry with some areas planted with conifers. You may spot saw pits near the path used in the days when the timber was sawn into planks in the woods, this being easier than transporting huge tree-trunks. This woodland is a good example of an area in which selective felling has taken place without any replanting of new beech. Most of the trees look decrepit and unhealthy in contrast to beech woodland you can see on Walks 2, 4 and 7.

After a time you will reach an unusual plantation of yew on the right of the path, yew being valuable as a furniture veneer timber. This track was once a lane which linked Bix Bottom and its church with Crocker End. On the left is a line of coppiced hazel, which marks the line of the old hedge, now surrounded by woodland. Further on you will see the line of the track, now grass covered, showing as a distinct ridge in the field.

2 SU714869

The path emerges over a stile on to a grassy field with a view of Soundess House to the right. This is a nineteenth-century building but earlier there was a house in this vicinity where Nell Gwyn, a favourite of Charles II is reputed to have lived. The lime trees in the parkland show a distinct browse line giving them a very manicured look where animals have eaten off the lower twigs.

Continue along the field edge with the hedge on your left until a stile is reached. Cross this and follow a track in front of the cottages. This hamlet is Crocker End and as its name implies was an area where pottery and bricks were made. As long ago as 1416 there was a thriving industry here when Thomas Stonor ordered 200000 bricks made by Flemish brickmakers from the kiln here to build the tower on the chapel at Stonor House. Families still exist in this area who have descended from these immigrants.

Follow the road along the right-hand edge of the common. Notice the characteristic shape of the common (easier on an OS map), its straggling shape becoming a funnel where crossed by roads.

After a short distance leave the road and take the track to the right side of a patch of woodland in front of more houses and continue in this direction for some distance.

The track follows the edge of Nettlebed Common where, for several centuries, there was a widespread brick, tile and pottery industry which lasted until 1938. The chalk here is capped with clay of a suitable type for firing and because of the plentiful supply of local wood for fuel the industry flourished. All trace of the kilns has now gone except one preserved in Nettlebed. The oldest kiln is thought to have been Soundess Kiln which was on the right of the track, now marked by several large ponds and hollows. All over the common traces of the clay diggings can be seen, many now forming ponds which are a valuable wetland habitat for plants, insects and amphibians in the generally well drained Chilterns. Many contain great reed mace, often erroneously called bullrush.

3 SU704874

When the trail reaches some cottages follow the path past The Cottage and Magpies Bungalow through an area of bracken with some heather. Bracken often spreads on such commons after overgrazing by animals or shading by encroaching trees.

The path crosses a bank marking the edge of the common and goes down through beech trees to a wide track where the trail turns right. Keep straight on and when a modern house is reached turn right down the side of it. (Look for an arrow on a telegraph pole.) The path continues over a stile beside a ha-ha, a disguised barrier between the garden and grazing animals. Continue down a narrow field bearing left across the little valley heading for a stile, to enter the woodland known as Berrick Trench. Follow the path along the ridge.

Replanting has been carried out here using mixed tree species. Notice how the grass is growing in these relatively open areas compared with the bare ground under the mature beech where the light conditions are poor. In grassy patches clumps of great mullein grow, their thick fleshy leaves covered with dense white downy hairs giving an easily recognizable felty appearance. Blue flowered nettle-leaved bellflower also grows here. Large spear thistles flower in June and July and are favourite food sources for red-tailed bumble bees and meadow brown butterflies. If you look carefully at some of the butterflies you may see tiny bright red lumps

St James' Church, Bix Bottom

Coppiced Ash stool

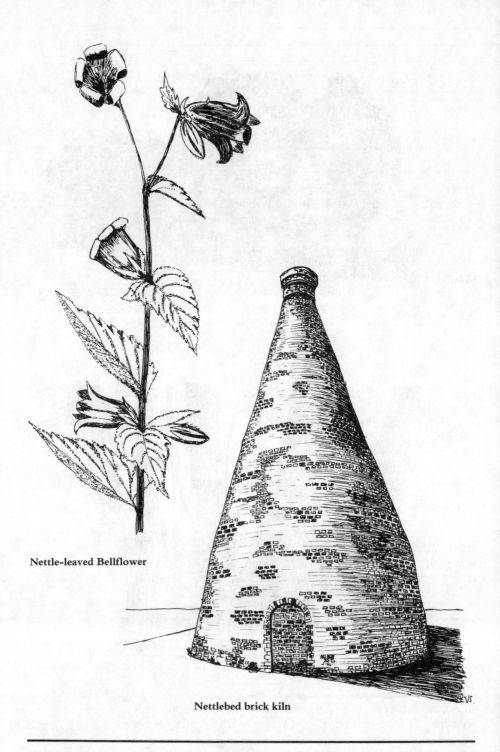

Nettle-leaved Bellflower

Nettlebed brick kiln

attached to their legs and bodies. These are parasitic mites sucking fluids from the body of their host; there may be several mites on one insect.

4 SU707884

At the edge of the wood follow the path almost straight on over a series of stiles, keeping the farm to the left-hand side, crossing small fields and a stony track.

SHORT CUT If you turn right here and follow this track along the valley bottom you will reach the Warburg Nature Reserve, owned by the Berks, Bucks and Oxon Naturalists Trust. At the far side you will see the interpretive centre with information on the reserve. Continue along the stony, then tarred, road back to the start at St James Church.

The trail climbs a grassy hill and drops into the valley through a small plantation. Climb a wide stile onto a track and turn left. Continue along the track which can be muddy.

In the past this formed part of the boundary of Minigrove (Maidensgrove) Manor and was another route more important in the past, leading to Cookley Green from Bix Bottom.

In the spring there is a marvellous display of flowers with wood anemones, bluebells, celandine and violets. Look out for the tiny green flower head of moscatel. Much of the hedge is coppiced hazel with yellow male catkins in early spring. In winter, brown rubbery ear fungus can be found, occuring mostly on elder, together with the hard black burnt-looking fungus with the descriptive name of King Alfred's Cakes.

After some distance a junction is reached. Turn right here up a steep stony holloway with foxgloves decorating the banks in summer. At the top there are wide views over the valley. Notice how many of the field corners have been planted with young trees, which will form good patches of habitat for wild woodland birds and butterflies as well as pheasants. The proximity of woodland plants in the nearby hedges should eventually result in the colonization of the new woodland by these species.

5 SU708891

When the track reaches the road, turn right. This hamlet is Russell's Water named after the Russell family who had a brick kiln here sometime prior to 1695, the industry closing at the end of the nineteenth century.

Keep along the road until Russell's Water Farm is reached where a narrow grassy path goes left onto the common opposite. Take this path and keep going parallel to the road.

It is plain to see how this vegetation is different from that occurring in the rest of the area. Bracken and heather grow here, plants that prefer acid soil as opposed to the chalk-loving species elsewhere. Silver birch is invading the disturbed heath, a forerunner of the natural woodland which would develop in time if left alone. Gorse, another typical invader, often flowers in winter, possibly a strategy to avoid predation by a small beetle whose larvae would eat the seeds produced by spring flowers. This heathy area, unusual in the Chiltern hills, shows well the effect of local soil types and conditions on the vegetation and adds variety to the wildlife which can be found.

As at Nettlebed there is a cap of Eocene Reading Clay here which is more suitable for bricks than the clay-with-flints deposited on many of the Chiltern hilltops. Again the pits and hollows are reminders of the clay-based industries here in the past.

Keep going in the same general direction as before and return to the road when the common changes to grassland. The boundary of the common on the right is an ancient one mentioned in a charter of Offa in 774 as a Greenway. It marked the boundary between the Hundreds of Ewelme and Pyrton, ancient administrative land divisions originally based on the area inhabited by a hundred families.

6 SU718886

At a sharp left bend in the road continue straight on over the grass until a lane is reached where the trail bears right. Follow the track heading downhill into woodland, although if you wish to visit the Warburg Nature Reserve the path signed at the top of the lane to the right leads down to the interpretive centre. Return to the start from here along the road to the left.

As you walk through the woodland look at the trees on the right. Many of them are deformed in shape after centuries of coppicing and pollarding as this is another part of Maidensgrove Common (known as the Scrubbs) where local people had rights to cut wood until the end of the nineteenth century. There are more woodland flowers here in spring particularly wood spurge and woodruff with its tiny white flowers and a ruff of leaves.

At a junction bear right following the track marked with an arrow. As you enter a more open area, where many of the trees have been cleared and replanted with saplings, notice how the flora changes with the extra light. The hedgerow alongside the path as you descend is full of flowers in early summer, many seedheads remaining visible throughout the winter; dark mullein, St John's wort and hedge bedstraw. Butterflies such as meadow brown, gatekeeper, marbled white and ringlets may be seen, feeding and basking in this sheltered patch.

Soon the path reaches the road where the trail turns left to return to the starting point at the church.

Coppiced Hazel bordering old trackway

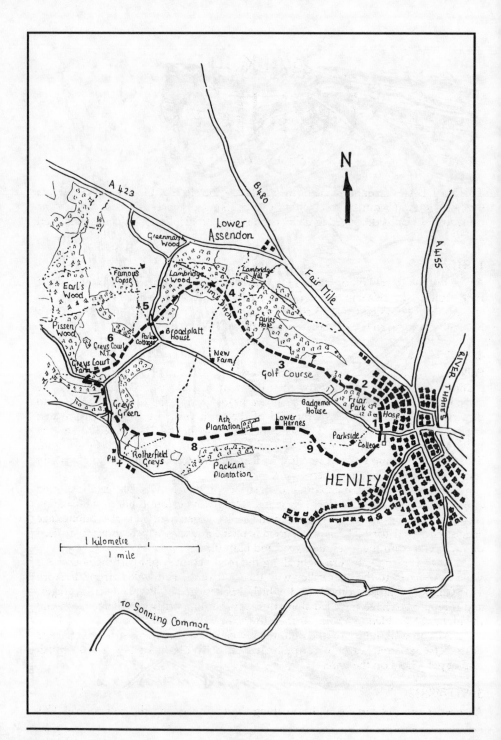

N

A 423

B 480

A 4155

Lower
Assendon

Fair Mile

Greenmans
Wood

Famous
Copse

Lambridge
Wood

Lambridge
Hill

Earl's
Wood

Grims Ditch

4

Fawits
Hole

5

Pissen
Wood

Greys Court
N.T.

6

Parks
Cottages

Broadplatt
House

New
Farm

RIVER THAMES

Greys Court
Farm

3

Golf Course

2

Badgemor
House

Friar
Park

Hosp.

1

7

Greys
Green

Ash
Plantation

Lower
Hernes

Parkside

College

P.H.

Rotherfield
Greys

8

Packam
Plantation

9

HENLEY

1 kilometre

1 mile

To Sonning Common

WALK 10

HENLEY

5.5 miles (9 km)

This walk passes through some of the old landscape close to Henley and highlights the wildlife which can be seen within easy walking distance of a busy town. The route follows paths described in Climenson's guide to Henley-on-Thames published in 1896.

1 SU756827

At the top of Gravel Hill turn into Hop Gardens. On the corner is the lodge of Friar Park, built in the 1890s in highly ornate French Flamboyant Gothic style. Turn left at the end of Hop Gardens and continue to the end of the houses until you reach a footpath climbing to the left beside a wire fence.

2 SU754831

Follow the path which crosses an open area where, in summer, many grasses can be found which can be told apart by their different shaped flowerheads. Later in the season when the seeds are ripe the flowerheads readily fall apart if handled, so dispersing the seeds. Towards the end of the walk compare this with cultivated grasses like barley or wheat. The seeds of these species have been bred to be very much bigger than the wild grasses, and when ripe do not fall out of the flowerhead. This means that the grain is not lost at harvest and has actually to be physically removed by the threshing process.

Numerous snails, often with brown stripes on the glossy shells, can be spotted amongst the nettles and on the grass stems. The yellow colours and brown banding serve to break up the snail's outline in the stalky vegetation, acting as camouflage against bird predators. This is also a good habitat for insects which, in summer, feed on the nectar from the roses, hogweed and brambles.

At the kissing gate turn right along the road. To the right past the houses is a wide view across to the river valley with the route of the Fair Mile in front. In April 1646 Charles I escaped from Oxford, which was besieged by Parliamentarian forces, and is reputed to have travelled along this way, turning off before Henley to spend the night at Hambledon Manor further down the Thames.

As you walk notice on the right the ivy climbing the rough-surfaced concrete posts between stretches of wire mesh. It climbs by means of tiny 'roots' which cannot get a hold on the wire.

3 SU748833

At a series of stiles carry straight on along the track crossing the golf course. This track follows the line of the boundary of a medieval deer park granted to John de Grey in 1311 and, amongst the line of trees, remnants of woodland flora such as dog's mercury, woodruff and sanicle can still be seen. Look out for a white sign which points across the fairway to the wood – watch out for golf balls at this point! When the wood is reached follow the path straight on.

In the spring this woodland is thickly carpeted with bluebells, followed later by patches of bracken which grow only on acid soil showing that here the chalk is covered by deposits of clay and flints. The ground is often covered with dry husks of empty beech mast. Although not occurring annually, in a 'mast' year huge amounts of seeds are produced but, however, there are very few seedlings and young trees to be seen. Many seeds are eaten by squirrels, birds and other animals, while germination can be difficult if the shoots become frosted or too dry. Seedlings are then vulnerable to more predation, again from squirrels as well as slugs and other invertebrates, so successful growth of a new beech is a chancy process.

As the trail passes through Lambridge Wood look out for wood rush with long, thin, shiny leaves fringed with white hairs and small brown flowers held in loose clusters at the end of the stem. Tiny white flowers on a delicate plant identify enchanter's nightshade.

4 SU739840

As the path curves to descend and then climb a small valley (where it can be muddy) you will see a marked bank on the left which continues through the woods for some distance. This is the line of Grim's Ditch which can be traced for about ten miles between Henley and Wallingford. It is thought to be an Iron Age boundary possibly between two types of settlement patterns, one using the still forested areas and the other cultivating lighter soil. The name Grim, which occurs at many similar sites in England, comes from the Old English word meaning evil spirits, who seemed to succeeding peoples to be the only possible builders of such impressive earthworks. In later centuries the ditch was used in many places as a road. Here it formed part of the Henley to Wallingford road, which was superceded in 1736 by the Henley Turnpike constructed to improve travel in the area, Henley being an important coaching centre with its river crossing.

Keep straight on along the path marked with yellow arrows as path 48 until a junction with path 32 is reached. Turn left here and continue through the woods until the road is reached. In this part of the wood you will see in places old stumps of large trees felled many years ago. In the Chilterns the traditional method of woodland management was to select the best and largest trees for timber and leave the smaller or unhealthy ones. This is one factor which has resulted in the poor state of much of the Chiltern beech woods today.

5 SU730838

Turn left on to the road and then immediately right along a track. Take the footpath which turns left before some large farm buildings between trees and a wire fence onto National Trust land. The path follows the field edge, through a gate and reaches a small bridge over a marshy area near a pond which is bordered with alders.

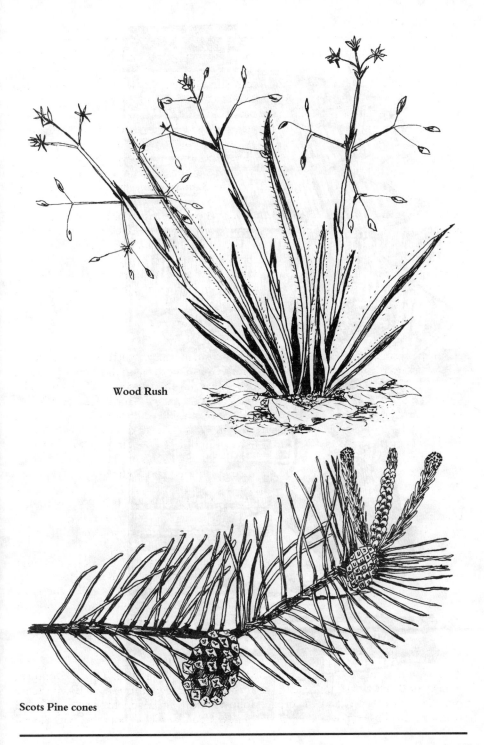

Wood Rush

Scots Pine cones

Prosper

Greys Court

As the path climbs slightly notice the massive oak tree beside the next stile. This is one of the many varied trees remaining from the landscaped park around Greys Court.

After another stile, look at the line of scots pines on the right. Several generations of female seed-bearing cones can be seen from the first year small pink cone to the third year woody grey cone ready to fall from the tree. Clusters of small yellow and brown pollen bearing male cones occur at the tips of many branches. Once the pollen has been shed these will fall off.

6 SU726833

Climb another stile into parkland. This deer park dates from before 1543 but the present park was probably landscaped much later when the fine specimen trees were planted. Sweet chestnut has diagonally ridged bark while horse chestnut can be identified from the candle shaped flowers in spring and the downward sweep of the branches in winter. These trees all have spreading branches because they have plenty of room and light. In woodland, trees tend to branch only near the top of the trunk and are not so easily identified by a distinctive shape.

Bear right through the National Trust entrance to Greys Court. The track passes in front of the buildings constructed over successive centuries. The land was held by the Grey family for four hundred years from the Norman invasion until it passed to the Crown after the Battle of Bosworth in 1485. It then came into the possession of the Knollys family who were related by marriage to Elizabeth I. The Stapleton family owned the house from 1724 to 1935 and it was given to the National Trust in 1969. The present sixteenth-century house, gardens and an unusual Tudor donkey wheel well-house can be visited. (Telephone 049 17 529 for details.)

Close to the road in front of the nearest building notice a tree with dark glossy leaves. This is a tulip tree so called because of its flowers. Both this and the nearby weeping ash appear on a print of Greys Court published in 1823.

The park road skirts the house and grounds and descends to a road where the trail turns left. Continue to the junction and take the right fork, crossing the road with care to walk alongside a sunken path amongst trees, a medieval holloway linking Greys Court to the church at Rotherfield Greys.

7 SU725829

As the road forks take the path which goes off to the left downhill through trees. Follow this path along the field edges over a series of stiles. If you look back up the valley there is a good view of Greys Court. The hedge along this edge contains a mixture of species and was probably formed when the surrounding woodland was felled many centuries ago, only a small remnant of woodland remaining on the right.

Along this stretch of the trail you are likely to see cereal crops. This is a chance to compare these cultivated members of the grass family with those you saw at the beginning of the trail. Observe how even-sized these plants are, a trait which has been specially bred to make for a more efficient harvest. Wild grasses have far more diversity in size.

8 SU736825

The path widens after it crosses through a gap in the hedge which is now on your left. Along this stretch look for flowers of knapweed, restharrow and bedstraw as well as pink dog roses and the white flowers of dogwood. Dogwood can be identified by the parallel pattern of the leaf veins and by its reddish stems, more obvious in winter.

A little further along the path there is a big patch of nettles which provide a habitat for the caterpillars of tortoiseshell butterflies. You might also see ladybird larvae feeding on aphids and nurse spiders who guard and protect their eggs and young in a dome-shaped web of thick silk found at the top of grass or other plants.

The path carries straight on passing through a patch of woodland called Ash Plantation before emerging near Lower Hernes Farm, whose buildings date from the seventeenth and eighteenth centuries.

Climb the stile and continue straight on through trees to another stile into a field. Follow the path along the edge of this field. On the hillside to the right ant-hills are clearly visible. Their size indicates that this land has been unploughed for many years. The pinkish flowered soft grass along the valley bottom is called yorkshire fog. In summer there are patches of blue germander speedwell and white lesser stitchwort.

Further on to the left the long grass provides a home for grasshoppers which can be heard during the summer months. The encroaching hawthorn and dogwood are good habitats for birds which like the dense cover of the bushes and the insect-rich grassland close at hand.

When you reach the stile, look back at the scrubby vegetation on the hillside. This hawthorn invasion, which probably results from seeds dropped by birds, is now taking over the grassland in the absence of grazing. If left alone this slope will gradually change to woodland.

9 SU748825

Over the stile carry straight on past the playingfields of Henley College. Over another stile the path becomes a track and, in early summer, you may be lucky enough to see house martins swooping down to a damp area, collecting mud for their nest building in house eaves.

Continue up the rough track bordered on the left by elm, which can be identified by the winged bark on the twigs. Bear left when the road is reached and you will return to the Gothic lodge house where the walk began.

Tower at Greys Court

Bibliografische Information der Deutschen Nationalbibliothek:

Die Deutsche Bibliothek verzeichnet diese Publikation in der Deutschen National-
bibliografie; detaillierte bibliografische Daten sind im Internet über http://dnb.d-
nb.de/ abrufbar.

Impressum:

Copyright © 2005 GRIN Verlag, Open Publishing GmbH
Druck und Bindung: Books on Demand GmbH, Norderstedt Germany
ISBN: 978-3-668-00538-9

Dieses Buch bei GRIN:

http://www.grin.com/de/e-book/301826/entstehung-auswirkungen-und-vor-und-
nachteile-von-massenproduktion-am

GRIN - Your knowledge has value

Der GRIN Verlag publiziert seit 1998 wissenschaftliche Arbeiten von Studenten, Hochschullehrern und anderen Akademikern als eBook und gedrucktes Buch. Die Verlagswebsite www.grin.com ist die ideale Plattform zur Veröffentlichung von Hausarbeiten, Abschlussarbeiten, wissenschaftlichen Aufsätzen, Dissertationen und Fachbüchern.

Besuchen Sie uns im Internet:

http://www.grin.com/

http://www.facebook.com/grincom

http://www.twitter.com/grin_com

Thema der Arbeit: Die Entstehung von Massenproduktion am Beispiel Ford

Titel der LV: Epochen der Wirtschafts- und Sozialgeschichte (C-1)

Inhaltsverzeichnis

1

1 Einführung

Bei meiner Hausarbeit über die Entstehung von Massenproduktion am Bespiel Ford
möchte ich nicht sofort mit der Betrachtung der Firma selber beginnen. Vielmehr soll
die Frage erörtert werden, weshalb es überhaupt zu einer solchen Produktionsform
gekommen ist. Welche Entwicklungen haben die Entstehung der Massenproduktion
überhaupt ermöglicht und welche Auswirkungen hatte dieses System auf die Beteiligten?

Um die Ursprünge der Massenproduktion zu verdeutlichen, werde ich daher zuerst
darauf eingehen, wie und warum sich die Marktorganisation im Laufe der Jahrhun-
derte überhaupt verändert hat und welche Auswirkungen das für den Arbeitsprozess
an sich aber auch für Menschen hatte. Da im diesem Zusammenhang vor allem der
Begriff der Arbeitsproduktivität zunehmend eine Rolle spielt, werde ich mich im darauf folgenden Teil der Hausarbeit mit einigen Überlegungen von Adam Smith, Frederick Winslow Taylor und natürlich Henry Ford zu diesem Thema befassen. Mit Hilfe
dieser Ausführungen werde ich dann die Entwicklung von der Fleißbandarbeit bis hin
zur Massenproduktion in der Firma Ford selber verdeutlichen. Um jedoch auch die
Chancen und Grenzen dieses Produktionssystems aufzuzeigen, arbeite ich ab-
schließend einige aus der Praxis resultierende Vor- und Nachteile der Massenproduktion heraus.

2 Die Ursprünge der Massenproduktion

Bereits im 15. Jahrhundert findet man arbeitsteilige Herstellungsprozesse, wie beispielsweise bei der Ausrüstung von Galeeren in Venedig, die während der Fahrt
durch die Kanäle erfolgte. Diese weisen jedoch noch nicht die typischen Merkmale
der Massenproduktion für Massenmärkte auf, da die Arbeitsabläufe weder zeitlich
getaktet waren, noch ein Fließband existierte.[1]

---

[1] Vgl. Bönig, J., Die Einführung der Fließbandarbeit in Deutschland bis 1933, Band 1, Münster, 1993, S. 42

2.1 Marktorganisation vor dem 18. Jahrhundert

Vor dem 18. Jahrhundert bestimmten strikt regulierte Märkte das Leben der Menschen, wobei besonders beachtenswert ist, dass das Wirtschaftssystem in das Gesellschaftssystem integriert war und nicht umgekehrt. Es existierten nur lokale Märkte und Wirtschaften, die jedoch nicht marktwirtschaftlich organisiert waren. Die dort gültigen Regeln dienten vornehmlich der Sicherstellung der Versorgung. Märkte waren nach dem Prinzip der Wechselseitigkeit und der Umverteilung organisiert, wobei der Austausch von Gleichwertigem im Mittelpunkt stand.[2]

Nicht nur der Tauschhandel war früher ein wichtiges Prinzip der Marktorganisation, sondern auch die Selbstversorgung und die damit verbundene Unabhängigkeit von Anderen. Der wichtigste Unterschied gegenüber der Reziprozität und der Redistribution war, dass eventuell vorhandene Überschüsse bereits auf den lokalen Märkten verkauft wurden. Das Ziel dabei war aber nicht nur die Erwirtschaftung eines Profits, sondern vor allem die volle Ausschöpfung der natürlichen Ressourcen.[3]

Da es zu dieser Zeit nur lokale Märkte gab, war das Gewinnstreben, wie es bei der Massenproduktion im Vordergrund steht, zweitrangig. Die vorhandenen Märkte unterlagen zwar Regeln der Marktorganisation, zielten aber nicht auf eine Massenproduktion ab. Der Übergang zur modernen Marktwirtschaft erfolgte erst im Laufe des 16. und 17. Jahrhunderts. Märkte, die vorher gesellschaftlichen Regeln unterlagen, wurden nun zu Märkten, die nach dem Gewinnprinzip funktionierten.

2.2 Von der Selbstversorgung zur bezahlten Arbeit

Weshalb erfolgte aber überhaupt ein Wandel von der Selbstversorgung zur bezahlten Arbeit? Die Selbstversorgung war hauptsächlich deshalb notwendig, damit die Güter des täglichen Bedarfs nicht am Markt beschafft werden mussten. Man muss sich nämlich darüber im Klaren sein, dass es nur lokale Märkte gab und nicht alle Güter

---

[2] Vgl. Polany, K., The Great Transformation. Politische und ökonomische Ursachen von Gesellschaften und Wirtschaftssystemen, Frankfurt am Main, 1995, S. 102
[3] Vgl. Schlude, U., Von den Geschäften der Fürstin, in: Forschung. Das Magazin der Deutschen Forschungsgemeinschaft, 2/2005, S. 23

des täglichen Lebens einfach vor Ort gekauft werden konnten. Um die Lebensgrundlage der Menschen zu sichern, war es also erforderlich das Prinzip der Autarkie aufrecht zu erhalten.

Erst später wurde der Fernhandel, der auch andere Städte einschloss, von Kaufleuten initiiert und die lokalen Märkte somit erweitert. Zu diesem Zeitpunkt bildeten sich die ersten Züge der kapitalistischen Marktwirtschaft heraus,[4] da nun viele Produkte am Markt erwerblich waren und eine Selbstversorgung nicht mehr zwingend nötig war.

Durch diese Entwicklung stand dem Markt plötzlich auch mehr Arbeitskraft zur Verfügung und tatsächlich entstanden in dieser Zeit, in der sich die ersten Industrien herausbildeten, auch die ersten Arbeitsmärkte.[5]

Allerdings wurde damals nicht nur Arbeit, sondern auch Boden und Kapital zu am Markt erwerblichen Gütern. Hier begünstigte insbesondere die Privatisierung von Grund und Boden nach und nach die Verarmung und Verschuldung der Bevölkerung,[6] so dass die Menschen auf dem Land sich nicht mehr selbst ernähren konnten. Zu diesem Zeitpunkt funktionierte das Prinzip der Autarkie praktisch nicht mehr und als Alternative bot sich nur die Arbeit in den neu entstandenen Industrien an. Die eigene Arbeitskraft, die bis dato der Selbstversorgung diente, wurde nun also zur bezahlten Arbeit.

2.3 Vom natürlichen Rhythmus zum geregeltem Arbeitstag

Die Menschen vor dem 18. Jahrhundert haben ihre Zeit aufgabenorientiert eingeteilt und ihre Tätigkeiten dem natürlichen Rhythmus angepasst. Die Zeiteinteilung war von der Natur und nicht von Uhren oder dem Takt der Maschinen vorgegeben.[7] Doch mit dem Wegfall der Selbstversorgung verlor die Bevölkerung auch die Selbstbestimmtheit was die Arbeitszeitorganisation betraf.

---

[4] Polany, K., a.a.O., S. 109 f.
[5] Ebenda
[6] Ebenda, S. 104 ff.
[7] Vgl. Thompson, Edward P., Plebeische Kultur und moralische Ökonomie. Aufsätze zur englischen Sozialgeschichte des 18. und 19. Jahrhunderts, Frankfurt/Main, 1980, S. 36 ff.

Warum jedoch wurde eine Umstellung überhaupt erforderlich? Wann wurde Arbeitszeit zum Messproblem? Die Umstellung wurde ganz offensichtlich erst erforderlich, als die Menschen nicht mehr für sich selbst sondern für andere zu arbeiten begannen. In diesem Zusammenhang stellt sich natürlich auch die Frage, weshalb die Bevölkerung diesen Wandel überhaupt mitgemacht hat, wo die Anpassung an diesen „unnatürlichen" Arbeitszeitrhythmus doch sehr schwer fiel. Tatsächlich hat die Bevölkerung sich dem neuen Arbeitsrhythmus nur widerwillig angepasst, konnte jedoch aus zahlreichen Gründen nicht am alten System festhalten.[8]

Vornehmlich ist hier zu nennen, dass das System der Selbstversorgung nicht mehr funktionierte und das Naturalsystem vom Pachtsystem ersetzt wurde. Die Menschen waren nun auf bezahlte Arbeit angewiesen und konnten zunächst im Rahmen der Heimarbeit ihren Arbeitsrhythmus auch noch weitgehend selbst bestimmen, solange die Ware zum vereinbarten Termin fertig wurde. Später jedoch, als die ersten Fabriken entstanden, die viel schneller, viel mehr als der Landarbeiter produzieren konnten, war die Existenzgrundlage in der Landwirtschaft für den Großteil der Bevölkerung endgültig verloren. Die Not trieb die Leute in die Fabriken und Betriebe, wo sie sich an die vorgegebenen Regeln halten mussten, um nicht ihre Arbeit zu verlieren.

Man erkennt an dieser Entwicklung deutlich, dass sich nicht nur das Verständnis von Arbeit sondern auch die Lebensverhältnisse geändert haben und mit der Arbeit in den Fabriken kam es so auch zum Übergang vom natürlichen Rhythmus zum strikt geregelten Arbeitstag. Das der Einsatz von Maschinen in den Firmen die Abkopplung von der natürlichen Arbeitszeit überhaupt erst ermöglichte, ist in diesem Zusammenhang ebenfalls vollkommen plausibel.[9] Doch auch das Gewinnstreben gewann dermaßen an Bedeutung, dass die Arbeit zeitlich getaktet werden musste, um Leerläufe jeglicher Art zu vermeiden.

---

[8] Ebenda, S. 39 ff.
[9] Ebenda, S. 44 f.

2.4 Die Praxis in den Betrieben

Um eine gleichmäßige Auslastung von Mensch und Maschine zur gewährleisten, wurde in den Betrieben nun wiederum die strikte Einhaltung der Arbeitszeit durch die Einführung von Uhren kontrolliert.[10] Folglich kam es also durch die Arbeit in den Betrieben nicht nur zur Trennung von Wohn- und Arbeitsstätte sondern vor allem auch zur strikten Trennung von Freizeit und Arbeitszeit.

Die Beschäftigten waren ihrerseits natürlich dazu gezwungen, sich an die von der Unternehmensleitung vorgegebenen Betriebsregeln zu halten, um ihr Überleben zu sichern. Dennoch gab es im 18. Jahrhundert auch Widerstände gegen diese hierarchische Kontrolle durch die Betriebsleitung, die sich beispielsweise in Phänomenen wie dem blauen Montag äußerten.[11]

Die Machtverhältnisse haben in den Betrieben generell eine wichtige Rolle gespielt. Das wird insbesondere deutlich, wenn man sich vor Augen führt, dass die Fabrikarbeiter vom Management sowohl zur genauen Einhaltung der Arbeitszeit als auch zur Erzielung einer höheren Arbeitsproduktivität angehalten wurden. Niedrigere Löhne waren nur ein Mittel der Firmenleitung die Arbeiter zur Zeit- und Arbeitsdisziplin zu erziehen. Es kam sogar so weit, dass der Autokrat Crowley schon im Jahre 1700 ein ganzes bürgerliches Gesetzbuch sowie eine Strafgesetzordnung anfertigte, um den Müßiggang seiner Arbeiter zu unterbinden.[12]

3 Die Revolutionäre

Mit der Frage, wie die Produktivität in den Betrieben gesteigert werden könnte, haben sich auch Adam Smith, Frederick Winslow Taylor und Henry Ford beschäftigt, auf die ich im Folgenden eingehen werde.

---

[10] Ebenda, S. 44
[11] Ebenda, S. 48
[12] Ebenda, S. 50

3.1 Adam Smith

Adam Smith beschrieb 1776 in seinem Werk „Der Wohlstand der Nationen" erstmals die Vorteile der Arbeitsteilung anhand des Beispieles einer Nadelfabrik. Insbesondere weist er auf die Tatsache hin, dass durch die aufeinander abgestimmten Arbeitsabläufe eine Produktivitätssteigerung erfolgt, wobei die Arbeiter für die Fertigstellung der Produkte keine besondere Ausbildung benötigen.[13]

Bei seiner Analyse kommt er zu dem Schluss, dass sich durch arbeitsteilige Prozesse die Arbeitsproduktivität, in Abhängigkeit vom Grad der Spezialisierung, von der Zeitersparnis und vom technischen Fortschritt, steigern lässt. Die Spezialisierung der Arbeiter bewirkt beispielsweise, dass sich der Einzelne nur auf einen Arbeitsauftrag beziehungsweise ein Arbeitsstück konzentrieren muss, wodurch er Routine bekommt. Da dadurch wiederum die Arbeitsschritte schneller erledigt werden können, wird so auch noch Arbeitszeit eingespart und somit eine höhere Arbeitsproduktivität erreicht. Ferner ist Smith der Meinung, dass die Arbeit mit Einzelteilen einen schnelleren technischen Fortschritt ermöglicht, weil diese leichter zu verbessern sind als komplexe Produkte.[14]

Außerdem stellt Smith sich die Frage, ob eine starke Arbeitsteilung im Hinblick auf die Marktsituation überhaupt sinnvoll ist. Smith ist der Meinung, dass der Grad der Spezialisierung auch von der Marktgröße abhängig gemacht werden muss. Ist ein Markt beispielsweise klein, dann ist eine spezialisierte Arbeitsteilung mit dem Ziel einer hohen Arbeitsproduktivität kontraproduktiv, da sowieso nicht genügend Güter getauscht bzw. verkauft werden können.[15]

Smith zeigt jedoch nicht nur die produktions- und absatzbezogenen Vor- und Nachteile der Spezialisierung auf, sondern weist auch auf die Folgen für die Arbeiter hin. Er hat bereits damals erkannt, dass die einfachen und monotonen Handgriffe unweigerlich zur Verdummung der arbeitenden Bevölkerung führen, da der eigene Verstand nicht mehr zur Lösung von Problemen eingesetzt werden muss.[16]

---

[13] Vgl. Smith, A., Der Wohlstand der Nationen, 10. Aufl., München, 2003, S. 9 - 10
[14] Ebenda, S. 19 ff.
[15] Ebanda, S. 9 ff.
[16] Ebenda, S. 662 ff.

Die dadurch entstehende Demotivation und Dequalifizierung der Arbeiter sind also auch Resultate der Trennung von durchführender und planender Arbeit und statt der Steigerung der Arbeitsproduktivität erfolgt dadurch ein Rückgang der selbigen.

3.2 Frederick Winslow Taylor

Zum Anfang des 20. Jahrhunderts entwickelte Frederick Winslow Taylor Smiths Ideen zur Arbeitsproduktivität dann zum sogenannten „Taylorismus" weiter, indem er einfache Arbeitsgänge mit dem Ziel industrieller Effizienz zerlegte, genau erfasste und organisierte.[17]

Ursprung von Taylors Überlegungen war die Leistungszurückhaltung der Arbeiter. Doch wie konnte man die Fabrikarbeiter bei gleichem Lohn zu mehr Leistung bewegen? Um die Motivation der Arbeiter und damit auch die Leistungsbereitschaft zu steigern, empfahl Taylor daher zum Beispiel die Einführung der leistungsorientierten Bezahlung.[18]

Eine weitere Grundvoraussetzung zur Steigerung der Arbeitsproduktivität war seiner Meinung nach, dass die Arbeit vom Management, basierend auf exakten Anleitungen, vorgegeben wird. Bei dieser Vorgehensweise sind dann beide Parteien, der Arbeiter und die Leitung, an der Lösung der Aufgabe beteiligt. Laut Taylor kommt das insbesondere den Arbeitern zugute, da sie nun nur noch die ausführenden Arbeiten zu erledigen haben und keiner Doppelbelastung mehr ausgesetzt sind.[19]

Er wollte damit erreichen, dass der Produktionsprozess vom Management und nicht von den Arbeitern gesteuert wird. Tätigkeiten, die vorher viele umfangreiche Kenntnisse erforderten, sollten nun vom Management geplant werden. Durch das fehlende Wissen über den Produktionsprozess wären dann auch die Arbeiter leichter austauschbar und in der Leistungszurückhaltung beschnitten.[20] Im Gegensatz zu Adam Smith lies Taylor jedoch die mögliche Demotivation der Arbeiter weitgehend unbeachtet.

---

[17] Vgl. Giddens, A., Soziologie, 2. Aufl., Graz/Wien, 1999, S. 337
[18] Vgl. Taylor, F. W., Die Grundsätze wissenschaftlicher Betriebsführung, München, 1919, S. 12 ff.
[19] Ebenda, S. 35 ff.
[20] Vgl. Müller, M., Taylorismus: Abschied oder Wiederkehr?, in: Mitbestimmung, 7/2000, S. 14

Dennoch kann man Taylor durchaus als Revolutionär bezeichnen, da eine derartig schematisierte Arbeitsteilung, wie er sie vorschlug, bis dato unbekannt war. Seine Ideen machte er sowohl durch Veröffentlichungen als auch durch Vorträge unter dem Begriff der „Wissenschaftlichen Betriebsführung" bekannt.[21]

3.3 Henry Ford

Die Prinzipien der Wissenschaftlichen Betriebsführung gewannen im Laufe der Zeit auch für Henry Ford eine wichtige Bedeutung. Im Gegensatz zu Taylor fokussierte Ford bei seinen Überlegungen allerdings nicht nur den Output sondern auch die Nachfragesituation. Als Resultat entstand letztlich das System der Massenproduktion, das auch als „Fordismus" bekannt wurde. Dahinter steht erstens die Idee der Entwicklung von Werkzeugen und Maschinen, die schnelle, präzise und einfache Arbeitsgänge zulassen und zweitens der Gedanke der exakten zeitlichen Taktung der Arbeit,[22] so dass die Produktion hoher Stückzahlen bei geringen Kosten möglich ist.

Die Einführung der strikten Arbeitsteilung sowie die daraus resultierende Fließarbeit und Massenproduktion erfolgte jedoch erst Jahre nach der Firmengründung. Zunächst lies auch Henry Ford von qualifizierten Arbeitskräften nur wenige Autos nach dem Auftragsfertigungsverfahren herstellen. Seine große Vision war jedoch, ein kraftvolles Auto zu entwickeln, das sich viele Menschen leisten könnten.[23]

---

[21] Bönig, J., a.a.O., S. 49
[22] Giddens, A., a.a.O., S. 337 - 338
[23] Vgl. Hounshell, D. A., From the American System to Mass Production. 1800 – 1932, in: Johns Hopkins University Press, Baltimore, 1984. Online im Internet: URL: http:// faculty.babson.edu/krollag//org_site/org_theory/barley_articles/hounshell_mass.html [06.01.2006].

4   Die Firma Ford

Die „Ford Motor Company" wurde 1903 bekannt,[24] wobei zu diesem Zeitpunkt weder mit Hilfe eines Fließbandes produziert wurde, noch große Mengen hergestellt wurden. Ford wollte zwar ein Produkt für die Massen bauen, durchlief aber ebenso wie andere Firmen einen Prozess, der vom Austauschbau über die Fließfertigung bis hin zur Massenproduktion führte.

4.1   Vom Austauschbau zur Fließfertigung

Neben der Automatisierung von Maschinen, ist vor allem der Austauschbau eine wichtige Vorraussetzungen für die Fließfertigung und somit auch für die Massenproduktion. Dieses so genannte "American System of Manufacture", das System der austauschbaren Teile, entstand gegen Mitte des 19. Jahrhunderts in den USA durch den Antrieb der Mechanisierung.[25]

Die Wurzeln des amerikanischen Systems des Austauschbaus finden sich in der Kleinwaffenindustrie wieder, wo erstmals Einzelteile bereits während der Produktion ausgemessen wurden. Die Waffenindustrie verbreitete nicht nur das Konzept der Austauschbarkeit, sie unterstützte auch die Entwicklung der dafür notwendigen Spezialmaschinen. Dennoch konnte sich das System der austauschbaren Einzelteile nur schwer etablieren.[26]

Warum aber verlief der Übergang zum Austauschbau überhaupt so schleppend? Zunächst einmal resultierte aus der Umstellung auf Spezialmaschinen kein höherer Gewinn, was auch als Grund für die langsame Einführung dieser interpretiert werden kann.[27] Darüber hinaus waren Einzelteile bis zur Jahrhundertwende, auf Grund der ungenügenden Präzision der Maschinen und der Differenziertheit der Rohstoffe, immer noch nicht austauschbar und mussten oft von Facharbeitern nachbearbeitet werden.[28] Letztlich kann man sagen, dass anfangs nicht einmal bekannte Waffenfir-

[24] Hounshell, D. A., a.a.O.
[25] Bönig, J., a.a.O., S. 47 f.
[26] Hounshell, D. A., a.a.O.
[27] Ebenda
[28] Bönig, J., a.a.O., S. 48 ff.

10

men wie Colt durch die Nutzung spezialisierter Maschinen und genauer Vermessung geringere Produktionskosten oder Austauschbarkeit erreicht haben.[29]

So gesehen macht es auch Sinn, dass die Firma Ford diese neue Produktionstechnik vergleichsweise spät eingeführt hat. Erst um die Jahrhundertwende machte Ford erste Rationalisierungsversuche, indem er seine Produktion verfeinerte. 1906/07 begann man bei Ford mit der Herstellung von austauschbaren Teilen für das Modell N. Notwendige Operationen der Teileherstellung waren auf Karten, gemäß den Grundsätzen der „Wissenschaftlichen Betriebsführung", detailliert beschreiben, so dass es keinen Bedarf an qualifizierten Fachkräften mehr gab.[30] Dadurch ließen sich die Produktionskosten und folglich auch die Produktkosten senken, was auch zu einer höheren Nachfrage führte.

Anfang 1913 war der Platz in der Fabrik bereits maximal ausgenutzt. Die Maschinen und Vorrichtungen waren nach Produktionsabfolge so dicht zusammengestellt und aufeinander abgestimmt, dass kaum noch Transportwege oder Leerzeiten entstanden. Doch weil die bisherige Arbeitsweise den möglichen Absatz von 200 000 Stück des Modell T's einschränkte, begann man auch bei Ford schließlich mit der Einführung von Fleißbändern, die eine noch effektivere Produktion ermöglichen sollten.[31]

Zunächst wurde bei Ford in der Teilefertigung eine Form der Fließarbeit eingeführt, bei der der Arbeiter das Werkstück selber weitergab. Der dafür geprägte Begriff der „moving assembly" war damit besetzt, dass der Zusammenbau während der Weitergabe der Einzelteile durch die Arbeiter erfolgte. Einen mechanischen Antrieb gab es zu dieser Zeit zwar noch nicht aber die Arbeitsproduktivität verbesserte sich dennoch erheblich. Alleine schon beim Zusammensetzen von Schwungradmagneten benötigte ein Arbeiter durch dieses System durchschnittlich nur noch 13 anstatt 20 Minuten.[32]

Nach eigenen Aussagen nahm Ford dann für die weitere Verfeinerung des Produktionsablaufes die Schlachthöfe von Chicago als Vorbild, wo bereits um das Jahr 1870 Transportbänder eingesetzt wurden, um die geschlachteten Tiere von Arbeiter zu

---

[29] Hounshell, D. A., a.a.O.
[30] Bönig, J., a.a.O., S. 52 ff.
[31] Ebenda, S. 55 ff.
[32] Ebenda, S. 61

Arbeiter zu befördern. Bei Ford wurde dieses Transportsystem, bei dem das Werkstück zum Arbeiter transportiert wird, im Februar 1913 in Form der ersten Fließlinie für den Abguss von Kleinteilen eingerichtet. Basierend auf genauen Zeitstudien konnten die einzelnen Arbeitsschritte so noch besser aufeinander abgestimmt und überwacht werden.[33] Bereits 1914 wurde dann die gesamte Anlage mit Fließbändern betrieben.[34]

4.2 Von der Fließfertigung zur Massenproduktion

Mit der ganzheitlichen Einführung von Fließbändern waren nun bei Ford die wichtigsten Voraussetzung für die Massenproduktion gegeben: der Platz in der Fabrik war optimal ausgenutzt und die Maschinenaufstellung orientierte sich an der Produktionsabfolge, so dass unnötige Transportwege vermieden wurden, die eingesetzten Spezialmaschinen bearbeiteten und überprüften die Einzelteile,[35] so dass die Fehlerquote geringer wurde und die Anlagen konnten von Hilfsarbeitern bedient werden, wodurch die Personalkosten gesenkt werden konnten.

Die häufigen Zeitstudien, die dann zusätzlich noch zur ständigen Verfeinerung der Arbeitsteilung dienten, ermöglichten eine Optimierung der Arbeitsproduktivität und exakte Leistungsvorgaben. Die Leerlaufzeiten wurden so für Mensch und Maschine minimiert,[36] was letztlich zur Massenproduktion bei gleichzeitig niedrigeren Preisen führte.

---

[33] Ebenda, S. 55 ff.
[34] Hounshell, D. A., a.a.O.
[35] Ebenda
[36] Bönig, J., a.a.O., S. 59 ff.

12

5 Die Chancen und Grenzen der Massenproduktion

Ford hatte mit seinem System der Massenproduktion zwar einen sehr großen Erfolg, doch anderseits haben sich auch zahlreiche Nachteile des Fordismus herauskristallisiert, die das System letztendlich zum Scheitern verurteilten.

5.1 Vorteile der Massenproduktion

Ford hatte bei seiner Entwicklung hin zum System der Massenproduktion natürlich hauptsächlich die Vorteile im Hinterkopf. So konnte zum Beispiel, durch die Einführung des Systems der austauschbaren Teile, die Prüfung der Einzelteile in den Arbeitsfluss integriert werden. Wie bereits Adam Smith erkannt hatte, ließen sich so auch Fehler kostengünstiger beheben, da nur das Einzelteil und nicht das gesamte Produkt neu bearbeitet werden musste.

Außerdem reduzierte sich durch die logische Anordnung der Maschinen der Platzbedarf und die Fertigungszeit. Die dadurch ebenfalls wegfallenden Transportwege minimierten darüber hinaus sowohl die Leerzeiten als auch Transportkosten, wodurch Ford sein Produkt sehr günstig anbieten konnte.

Ford orientierte sich auch an Taylors Ideen, indem er die Arbeit in kleine Aufgaben teilte und diese anhand von präzisen Arbeitsanleitungen durchführen ließ. Dadurch konnte die Arbeit nicht nur besser vorbereitet, sie konnte auf Grund der starken Spezialisierung nun auch von ungelernten Arbeitskräften durchgeführt werden. Die sinkenden Personalkosten und der gleichzeitige Anstieg der Produktion resultierten natürlich auch in niedrigeren Preisen und einem höheren Absatz.

Ein weiterer Vorteil der Massenproduktion ist darüber hinaus die Zeitersparnis. Im Vergleich zu anderen Fertigungsverfahren können die Produkte bei diesem System nämlich wesentlich schneller hergestellt werden. Da daher viele Kunden gleichzeitig bedient werden können, wird also auch der gesamte Vertrieb erleichtert. Vorraussetzung hierfür ist natürlich ebenso der Herstellung hoher Stückzahlen, da erst eine hohe Produktionsmenge den Verkauf zu günstigen Preisen zulässt.

13

Zusammenfassend kann man also sagen, dass die Einführung der Massenproduktion bei Ford für eine optimale Nutzung der vorhandenen Ressourcen steht. Seinen
Vorstellungen entsprechend hat er es geschafft, seine Gesamtkosten so stark zu op-
timieren, dass er ein Massenprodukt herstellen und zu einem günstigen Preis verkau-
fen konnte.

5.2 Nachteile der Massenproduktion

Vielfach hat Ford allerdings nicht die Probleme, die bereits Adam Smith angedeutet
hat, bedacht. Beispielsweise mussten sich die Fabrikarbeiter bei der Massenproduktion, im Austausch für einen eigenen Arbeitsplatz, an die exakt vorgegebenen und
monotonen Betriebsabläufe halten. Dadurch, dass sie nur noch für die ausführenden
Arbeiten zuständig waren verloren sie ihre Selbstbestimmtheit und genau das führte
auch zu einer geringeren Arbeitsproduktivität.

Darüber hinaus führte die extreme Belastung durch das Akkordlohnsystem, auf
Grund der gesundheitlichen Folgen, zu mehr Fehlzeiten und Kündigungen. Weiterhin
entwickelte sich dadurch auch eine starke Personalfluktuation, die Ford trotz hoher
Löhne und Prämien nicht eindämmen konnte.[37]

Aus wirtschaftlicher Sicht lässt sich als Nachteil der Massenproduktion die Unflexibili-
tät des Systems nennen. Durch den Einsatz von Spezialmaschinen und deren fest-
gelegte Reihenfolge ist bei einem Produktwechsel nicht nur die Stilllegung der Produktion, sondern auch der Umbau sämtlicher Maschinen nötig. Da es sich größten-
teils um Spezialmaschinen handelt, muss der größte Teil des Inventars sogar ver-
schrottet werden. Eine schnelle Reaktion auf Nachfrageschwankungen ist bei diesem
Produktionssystem also praktisch ausgeschlossen. Erschwerend kommt noch hinzu,
dass der gesamte Produktionsprozess bei Maschinenausfällen zum Stillstand kommt,
da die einzelnen Arbeitsprozesse aufeinander aufbauen.

Ein weiterer Nachteil ist, dass Fließbanderrichtungen leicht nachzuahmen sind, was
von vielen Unternehmen auch gemacht wurde. Für bereits nach diesem System pro-
duzierende Unternehmen bedeutet das mehr Konkurrenz und für diejenigen, die das

---

[37] Bönig, J. a.a.O., S. 64 ff.

14

Produktionssystem einführen, hohe Kapitalbindungskosten auf Grund der vielen Spezialmaschinen. Aus Letzterem resultiert wiederum eine starke Einschränkung für neue Investitionen und somit auch für den gesamten Bereich von Forschung und Entwicklung.

6 Schluss

Stellt man sich nun noch einmal die Frage, wie es überhaupt zur Entstehung der Massenproduktion kommen konnte, dann kann man als Grund zunächst die Veränderung der Organisation der Märkte nennen. Einerseits hat der Wandel von der Selbstversorgung zum marktwirtschaftlichem System Arbeitskräfte frei gesetzt, andererseits hat das Pachtsystem zur Verarmung der Bevölkerung geführt, was die Menschen überhaupt erst in die Zwangslage gebracht hat in den neu entstandenen Fabriken arbeiten zu müssen.

Die in den Betrieben vorherrschenden hierarchischen Strukturen und exakten zeitlichen Vorgaben durch die Unternehmensleitung waren wiederum der Grundstein für die Entstehung des Fordismus. Durch die ständige Kontrolle und Korrektur des Produktionsprozesses ist bei der Firma Ford dann im Laufe der Zeit die Massenproduktion entstanden.

Die Auswirkungen dieses Systems auf die beteiligten Fabrikarbeiter hat Ford jedoch ganz einfach unterschätzt. Offensichtlich hat er nämlich nicht damit gerechnet, dass die monotonen und vom Management genau vorgeschriebenen Arbeitsabläufe die Fabrikarbeiter in eine derartig ausgeprägte Sinnkrise manövrieren und so starke gesundheitliche Auswirkungen haben, dass es sich letztlich auch auf den Produktionsprozess auswirkt.

Dennoch konnte Ford seine Vision verwirklichen: er hat es als erster geschafft ein Luxusgut, dass sich zunächst nicht viele Menschen leisten konnten,[38] so günstig zu produzieren, dass es für die Massen erschwinglich wurde. Damit hat er sich sozusagen einen vollkommen neuen Markt, einen Anbietermarkt für das Produkt „Auto", geschaffen, auf dem sein Erfolg basierte.

---

[38] Ebenda, S. 52

An seine Grenzen ist dieses System erst gestoßen, als die Entwicklung vom Verkäufer- zum Käufermarkt erfolgte und die Abnehmer individuellere Ansprüche an Autos stellten. Das konnte durch das starre Produktionssystem von Ford nicht bewältigt werden, so dass auch er nach neuen Alternativen für sein System der Massenproduktion suchen musste.

16

7 Literaturverzeichnis

Bönig, J., Die Einführung der Fließbandarbeit in Deutschland bis 1933, Band 1, Münster, 1993, S. 42 ff.

Giddens, A., Soziologie, 2. Aufl., Graz/Wien, 1999, S. 337 ff.

Hounshell, D. A., From the American System to Mass Production. 1800 – 1932, in: Johns Hopkins University Press, Baltimore, 1984. Online im Internet: URL: http:// faculty.babson.edu/krollag//org_site/org_theory/ barley_articles/hounshell_mass.html [06.01.2006].

Müller, M., Taylorismus: Abschied oder Wiederkehr? in: Mitbestimmung, 7/2000, S. 14 ff.

Polany, K., The Grat Tranformation. Politische und ökonomische Ursachen von Gesellschaften und Wirtschaftssystemen, Frankfurt am Main, 1995, S. 102 ff.

Schlude, Ursula: Von den Geschäften der Fürstin, in: Forschung. Das Magazin der Deutschen Forschungsgemeinschaft, 2/2005, S. 23 ff.

Smith, A., Der Wohlstand der Nationen, 10. Auflage, München, 2003, S. 9 ff.

Taylor, F. W., Die Grundsätze wissenschaftlicher Betriebsführung, München, 1919, S. 7 ff.

Thompson, Edward P., Plebeische Kultur und moralische Ökonomie. Aufsätze zur englischen Sozialgeschichte des 18. und 19. Jahrhunderts, Frankfurt/Main, 1980, S. 35 ff.

9 783668 005389